HUGH JACKMAN
AND THE
JOY REVOLUTION

HUGH JACKMAN
AND THE
JOY REVOLUTION

CREATING WILD SUCCESS
BY DOING WHAT YOU LOVE

Louisa Joy Dykstra

Cover design by Rachmad Agus

I have no official connection with Hugh Jackman or Deborra-lee Furness.
The information about their life came mostly from recorded audio and video
interviews (although I learned I can't always trust Hugh's memory for dates). ☺
Some details could only be found in print, so their accuracy depends on someone
else capturing quotes and facts correctly.

ISBN 978-1-0968-0352-2

This book is dedicated to my kids: Kyle, Blake, and Joanna
May your lives be full of Joy.

This is also a love letter to Deb and Hugh.
If I were writing fiction I couldn't create two characters I love more.
Thanks for being who you are
and being a shining model of living with Joy.

This project would never have reached the finish line without
encouragement from Dana Wilde and Sonia Garrett
and research help from Sue Bueti.
I am forever grateful.

TABLE OF CONTENTS

WHO "SHOULD" READ THIS BOOK?

We have an epidemic of mom guilt.

You should read to your infant at least 20 minutes a day. You should cook locally-sourced, in-season meals. And your kids should magically eat them. You should provide exposure to the arts and plenty of outdoor free play. But your kids should never be out of your sight. You should do weekly date nights. You should "lean in" at your job. You should run the PTA's fundraiser. Oh, and you should always take time for yourself so you can remain calm and positive through it all.

Yowza! Anyone else tired of all the *shoulds*? I have good news; this is the book that helps you *untangle the knot of shoulds* in your head, because all of us have a few things on the list above that we are good at and love to do, but we don't all need to do it all!

Everyone has different natural strengths. When we push ourselves to do things we hate or aren't good at or don't really care about, we get frustrated and wonder why we constantly feel like we're failing. When we each do what we're best at—what comes most naturally to us—we accomplish way more—we ENJOY life way more—and that gives us the confidence to try new things and expand what we're good at! AND the world thrives because of our joy!

In fact, I propose abolishing the phrase "guilty pleasure." Pleasure is a strong motivator. Pleasure creates efficiency. Pleasure makes your brain work better! Pleasure is your superpower.

You may be thinking, "Girl, that's crazy talk! If I only did things that brought me joy, my life would be a disaster!" That's because you don't yet know how to use your autopilot brain to your advantage. This book will show you how.

By the way, this doesn't only apply to moms. If you're a grandpa, a business owner, a teenager, a new retiree, an elected official, a teacher, or anyone else who's feeling the weight of a lot of *shoulds*, this book is for you, too.

This is the story of how going with the flow of my fascination with Hugh Jackman, spending hours and hours watching interviews with him just because I was enjoying it so much, led to understanding brain science and emotions in a new way, which led to big improvements in my business, my marriage, and my health. And that led to me deciding to put it all together into an easy guide for you to join me in living what I call *the Joy Revolution*!

And you get to learn a lot about Hugh in the process. You know what his least favorite word is? Should.

Does that sound FUN to you? If so, this book is for YOU!

And you know what? You even get to decide HOW you read it. If you picked it up primarily to learn more about Hugh Jackman, you can skip right to Part II, I won't tell. Or if you want to jump right in with living the Joy Revolution yourself, you can start with Part I to get the basics, then skip to Part III to get some specific ideas. You can always come back and read about Hugh when you're in the mood. (See? No *shoulds* here!)

Now take a deep breath... and come with me on a joyful journey!

PART I
MY JOY REVOLUTION

CHAPTER 1

WHAT DOES HUGH HAVE TO DO WITH THIS?

Hugh didn't start the Joy Revolution. Joseph Campbell told us to follow our bliss. Abraham Hicks tells us joy is the key. Dana Wilde tells us to feel good first, then take action.

But Hugh, through the movie *The Greatest Showman,* brought the Joy Revolution into pop culture. In addition to all the adults inspired by the movie to wake up to new possibilities, it's world-changing to have a generation of kids growing up singing about their dreams and about proudly being your authentic self. As Hugh said, "It's a movie about family and joy and optimism and being who you are, and that is a journey that is ongoing for everybody, me included."

What do I mean by the Joy Revolution?

For many years our culture has placed the highest value on things like hard work and sacrifice and meeting other people's expectations. But we're shifting to an understanding of the power of Joy: that doing what you love is the surest path to success, that happiness has powerful implications for our health, and that trusting joy leads us into the fullness of who we are and thus our strongest potential for impacting the world.

The Joy Revolution is **not** about pretending to always be joyful, nor about trying to create a life where everything is perfect. It's about listening to what your emotions tell you, and about being more YOU, because when you shine, you light up the world! As Abraham Hicks says, when your gas gauge is empty, don't put a happy face sticker over it. Fill it up!

Hugh's name is in the title, but this is really the story of what I've learned from Hugh and his wife, Deborra-lee, as a team. They each had been living the Joy Revolution in their own way, but together they have become a powerful force for good in the world. Here are a few examples of how Hugh describes Deb's role in their journey:

> *If I was not with Deb the last 20 years I'd be a very boring person. Deb has completely changed who I am in many, many ways. Deb knows how to live life to the full every day.*

> *Deb is way more vivacious, gregarious, outgoing... I have become infinitely more confident, infinitely braver, and more within myself from being with Deb. She trusts herself implicitly. She is fearless about everything she does in life. She doesn't care what other people think. It is a compulsion for her to act from her heart.*

> *If you know her Mum at all, too, you'll know that it's sort of in the genes. This is a formidable family who somehow change the world and make everyone happy about it!*

This is not a typical biography. While it does include a lot of details about their life, it's intertwined with my own story and my observations, and puts all that together into a road map you can use to join the Joy Revolution!

You see, my life changed when I saw *The Greatest Showman* the first time.

I had been a student of positive thinking and brain science for eight years or so. But I only went to see the "the new circus movie" because my daughter trains in aerial and circus arts, and she wanted to join her instructors in going to see it together. I was a little reluctant because I don't love the history of how circuses have treated animals. (All the animals in the movie are animated, by the way.)

And there, on the screen, was a beautiful parable that summarized everything I had learned about happiness and brain power and vision, wrapped up in this gorgeous package of costumes and dancing and sticks-in-your-head music and JOY!

Hugh hadn't really been on my radar, me not exactly being the target demographic of *X-Men*. If asked about him, I would have said, "Oh, the guy from *Kate & Leopold*? Yes, he's cute." At my first viewing of *Showman* my mind was blown. I left the theater with many questions. Since when can

Hugh Jackman dance like that? Is that really him singing? (I had completely missed his Broadway career.)

So I Googled "does Hugh Jackman sing Greatest Showman" (because in past movie musicals, often times the actor on the screen was lip syncing the songs.) Everything I read led me to learn more, to keep going deeper with interviews about the making of the movie. My daughter and I saw the film four more times in the following week, and I gave my entire team a New Year's assignment to see the movie and get the soundtrack.

As I continued learning about the eight year journey to get the movie made, I started watching more and more interviews with Hugh about other things as well. Before long, I started to realize that while the subject of the movie was ostensibly P.T. Barnum, the message, especially of the songs, was 30% Barnum and 70% Hugh and Deb. I'm still learning something new every day from watching how they live. It's been life changing. Here are a few highlights as a preview:

- I love their underlying philosophy of "Have a go!" They've gotten where they are by being eager to try anything that intrigues them, along with a huge helping of going ALL IN to whatever they decide to try.
- Family truly comes first. How they do marriage has really inspired me.
- I've learned a lot from them about how to gracefully handle being in the public eye – how to balance authenticity and privacy.
- My favorite is that they uplift people. Whether Hugh is working a line of screaming fans at a movie premiere or interacting with paparazzi or shoveling manure in Africa, he SEES people and honors them.

But probably the most impactful thing I learned is the trickiest for me to articulate. "Studying" Hugh completely changed my self-image.

In fact, when I started making notes about how Hugh was inspiring me, the working book title in my head was *Hugh Jackman is My Personal Trainer.* But then people would have been looking for details of Hugh's workouts and nutrition plan, and this is definitely not that book. There is plenty of information about that online – all about 1000 pound weight-lifting clubs and thousands of pounds of chicken breasts. I also got concerned the title would be an invitation for Hugh to give me a challenge like he did his mate-since-kindergarten, Gus Worland, to run the New York Marathon. Not going to happen. ☺

Plus I would have had to add *And My Marriage Counselor. And My Business Coach.* And let's face it, that's getting way too clunky for a book title. *Joy Revolution* covers it all.

I grew up in a very conservative household (no makeup, no jewelry, limits on what we wore) so I always felt like a bit of an ugly duckling. When I went to college I put on the usual "Freshman 15" and have felt self-conscious about my body shape ever since. My first marriage didn't help. After asking me to marry him, my fiancé said I should lose 10 pounds before we took our engagement photos. Of course knowing what I know now I would have immediately run far, far away from that relationship, but that's another book entirely.

How did Hugh change me? A reporter said to him, "You change bodies the way other actors change costumes." A light bulb went on in me. Your body, your hair, those things are not who you are. They are the costume you currently present to the world, but they are not the essence of YOU. You may think, "Duh." But to me, after years of judging my physical imperfections as character flaws, it was revolutionary.

Very few people in the world are willing to go to the lengths Hugh does in sculpting his costume, inside (muscles) and out (hair and beard). One of the reasons he has been extremely successful in that pursuit is that he believes he CAN do anything he puts his mind to. The ever-changing facial hair grows in his sleep. The muscles, not so much.

What sealed the deal of my changed body image is Hugh's clear adoration of Deb, who makes no pretense about her exercise philosophy. "I haven't got that discipline. I just want to have fun." When asked in an interview if she'd ever auditioned for a role she knew wasn't right for her, she told about when her agent convinced her to try for a part as an anorexic woman. "I'm chubby. I could never pull that off." (I wouldn't call her chubby but I love that she doesn't define herself by her shape.) Their rock solid marriage is a big part of what moved them into the hero category for me. From Deborra-lee I got a new life goal: to someday be referred to as a Humanitarian. Oh, and I added a Disruptor Award to my bucket list, too.

Common misconceptions about Joy

Before I go any further, I want to clear up some common misconceptions about joy, related to **hard work** and **fear**.

Trusting Joy does NOT mean sitting around doing nothing. People who live in Joy usually accomplish ASTOUNDING things. (Exhibit A: Hugh) The difference is, they don't take action from a place of resentment or dread or obligation. They find a way to feel good about what they're doing, or they do something different. You probably won't hear them say, "This is so hard!" More likely it would be "This might take everything in me, but I think I can do it, and I'm excited to jump in!" or "Hmmm, this isn't flowing. Better take a step back and see if there's a better way."

And what about fear? People who Trust Joy know the difference between fear that tells them to avoid something (like walking alone on a dark street) and a different kind of fear that has a component of thrill, which spurs them to prepare in every way they can... then leap!

Trusting Joy doesn't hold you back from greatness, it propels you toward it.

So how does the Joy Revolution work?

CHAPTER 2

THE JOY REVOLUTION GUIDE

There are only two things you need to know in order to live a Joy-led life:

1. **What do I want?**
2. **How do I feel?**

Simple, right? Here's the catch. When you ask yourself those two questions, you might get a jumbled mess of conflicting self-talk.

What if I don't even know what I want?
I thought I'm supposed to be content with what I have?
If I focus on what I want, that's selfish!
Most days all I feel is exhausted and overwhelmed.

In fact, this confusion is so prevalent in our culture, we think "good" parenting is teaching kids they can't have what they want and they shouldn't be upset about it. Even the Rolling Stones tried to convince us, *You Can't Always Get What You Want.* Stop it! When you're taught not to follow your instincts about what you want and how you feel, life is so much harder than it needs to be.

So while following things that bring you joy is truly simple, there are some important nuances that make it work. The magic of living the Joy Revolution is getting good at finding clarity on both those questions in any given moment.

Let's break it down.

What do you want?

1. *Wanting things means you're alive!*

The first belief you may need to reprogram is understanding it's okay, even healthy, to want things! You solve problems, invent new things, and start businesses when you want more. If the word "want" feels uncomfortable to you right now, think of it as your purpose. Just realize that wanting more is part of being ALIVE. It's how you're designed.

2. *You can practice gratitude AND want more.*

As a child you probably received the message, "You can't have that thing you want, because you should be grateful for what you already have." That's a simple misunderstanding of what wanting means. You can, and do, "want" things you already have – that's the definition of appreciation! Your sweet spot is appreciating what you have AND having a clear vision of what you want next. So yes, start with appreciation—the things you love about your home, the things you love about your partner, the strengths of your kids, what you enjoy about your coworkers, and—most importantly—things you love about *yourself*. Those are all things you want, that you already have! Then begin articulating what you want next. You'll feel both satisfied and excited!

PLAY ALONG: Grab a notebook and pen, then set a timer for 4 minutes and write a continuous stream-of-consciousness brainstorm of things you want. Remember to include things you want that you already have. You may be surprised what comes out!

3. *Your unique wants are your gift to the world.*

This is a huge key. I'm not talking about things you feel you *should* want. I'm talking about you, in your deepest heart of hearts... what *you* want. Sometimes it takes a while to clear off years of striving to meet other people's expectations to uncover what YOU truly want. It's worth it. Because that's where you'll shine!

You can tell what your unique gifts are by how you spend your time when no one is telling you what to do. You can tell by what you joke about. "I wish I could get paid for..." In contrast, you can tell when you're focused on external expectations by being aware of **two red-flag "s" words:** ***should*** **and** ***supposed to***. Anytime you catch yourself saying those words, stop and get clarity. Is this something I really care about? Is this something I want to do? Is there any possible way I could get to the desired outcome other than me doing what I just said I "should" do? Is this really my highest priority right now? Sometimes all it takes is a quick shift to more empowering words like "I want to..." or "I'm considering..." And sometimes it's something you really don't want to do.

It made a huge difference for me when I (finally!) stopped thinking I *should* get good at meal planning and cooking, and decided to spend time on the things I really wanted to do – like researching public education policy so I could be a strong citizen advocate, and learning more and more about Hugh and Deb so I could share my observations in a book about Joy! There is magic in learning to trust what you're drawn to and the message it has for you. Instead of beating myself up, I can help someone else "monetize her Pinterest habit" by paying her to plan meals and shop and cook for us.

By the same token, if cooking is your favorite creative outlet, or your dream job is homeschooling your kids, don't listen to the voices saying you *should* want something different! When you feel lit up inside, no matter what you're doing, you ARE changing the world, probably in ways you can't imagine yet.

You have probably been told that focusing on what you want is selfish. But what's the rule when you get on an airplane? You HAVE to put on your own oxygen mask first before helping others. When you're trying to be what others want you to be, you don't have as much to give because you're not filling your tank. Plus, you're depriving the world of the unique gifts you bring to the table!

PLAY ALONG: Take a look at the list you made. Is there anything you want to cross off because although you feel you should want it, you're not sure you really do? Anything you want to add that you didn't write before because you felt you shouldn't want it?

4. State what you want instead of what you don't want.

Getting clarity on what you *don't* want can be a helpful step, but then it's hugely important to flip it around to articulate what you *do* want.

What you want has to be stated in the positive, because your brain thinks in pictures. If I tell you there is no pink elephant in my office, what picture pops into your head? If you don't want your kids to be whiny, then state that in the form of, "I want to have more joyful interaction with my kids."

Why is it important to know that your brain thinks in pictures? Because your brain is a *powerful* tool in creating what you want. There is a filter (it's called the Reticular Activating System if you want to get technical) that determines what you notice and remember. That filter literally lets in *things that match the pictures already stored* in your brain. So if the primary picture in your brain is that your kids are too whiny, you will notice every second of whining and you will literally not notice or remember your kids' sunnier moments. The more you notice and comment on their whining, they'll come to believe they are whiners, and their Reticular Activating Systems will notice more things to whine about! Seriously!

Are you starting to see why this is such important knowledge? **Because that one piece of information is worth the price of the book right there.** Always state what you DO want. You can use this in parenting, in your relationships, in your job, and in your self-talk. When you say, "Don't touch that!" what your child's brain processes, as a mental picture, is reaching out and touching that! So an instruction like "Hands behind your back!" in front of a hot stove or something breakable gives toddlers a higher chance of success. (For a much more in-depth study of the brain, check out *Train Your Brain* by Dana Wilde.)

We all have had a tendency to focus on problems because we have been trained that problem-solving is a worthy skill. If you flip your perspective and call it solution-finding, putting your focus on the way you want things to be instead of digging into the problem, your brain will come up with solutions much more quickly and efficiently.

Let's add **two more red flag "s" words** to your awareness: *struggling* **and** *stuck*. Whenever you catch yourself saying or thinking those words, stop and reframe. State the subject in terms of what you *do* want, and substitute words like "I'm going to focus on…" or "I hope…" You'll be AMAZED at the difference it makes!

PLAY ALONG: Look again at your list. Is there anything you stated as what you don't want? Take a minute to rewrite it in terms of what you do want.

5. *Reprogram your autopilot with techniques like visualizing*

Once you're clear on what you want, amplify it. Visualizing is also known as dreaming. Dreaming is the word Hugh and *The Greatest Showman* use, but to be clear, we're talking about much more than random daydreaming.

Let's once again look at the brain science.

Only 5% of your brain is conscious, the other 95% is your autopilot brain (my own term, not a technical one). Most of us only learn how to use the conscious part, but OH MY GOODNESS you unlock power when you learn how to intentionally use the autopilot part.

Your autopilot brain runs your basic biology, but that's not all. Think about when you first learned to drive a car. It took so much conscious concentration! *Let's see, I go 15-20 mph when making a left turn, 5-10 mph making a right turn. I'm about 100 feet before the stop sign, so now is when I turn on my blinker and start to slow down.* Once you're comfortable driving, you have large chunks of time where you're not consciously aware of driving at all, and that's ok! Your autopilot brain has taken over!

Impulses, urges, cravings, reactions, all of those come from your autopilot brain. How does your autopilot get programmed? The messages you heard when you were a kid are part of it. But what's the biggest thing that keeps programming new patterns? Drum roll please... your SELF TALK.

The reason you may have decided you can't trust your instincts is that your autopilot brain is focused on what you *don't* want! Your autopilot is steering you straight into a snowbank, so you live life constantly trying to override it. The whole concept of willpower is overriding your autopilot. And you know what? It gets EXHAUSTING. Wouldn't it be MUCH easier to reprogram where the autopilot is pointed??

Comfort zone is another word for autopilot programming. When people tell you to get out of your comfort zone, they are literally telling you to override your autopilot. But it is SO much more efficient (and has a higher success rate) to learn instead to reprogram your autopilot, which I call *expanding your comfort zone.*

Visualization is one technique you can use to reprogram your autopilot brain and create change in your life. The reason change can feel hard is when your self-talk is focused on what you've always done, your autopilot brain recreates the same life each day. When you invest time visualizing, you reprogram what you *feel like* doing (and eating and saying). Really! Here, I'll let Hugh give you detailed instructions, as he shared with a group of entrepreneurs in 2018.

> *I've found the best time to actually invest in that imagin-*
> *ation, or in dreaming—this could be anything, this could be*
> *about your kids, your family, your job, anything—is just*
> *before I go to bed. I used to have the TV on or read in that*
> *time before lying down and falling asleep, but that's when I*
> *feel it's the strongest time. Almost just before you go off to*
> *sleep, that dream-like state, is the best time to really*
> *imagine. When I say imagine, it's like an actor imagines*
> *make-believe. Smell it, hear it, hear the sounds of voices*
> *around you, picture it clearly, 100%. The clearer the film in*
> *your head as you go off to sleep, the more real it will be when*
> *it comes true.*

Those clear mental pictures reprogram your autopilot, especially while feeling the emotion and using all your senses. Other reprogramming techniques include journaling, mantras, and vision boards. But you might as well start with what Hugh uses, don't you think? *#whatwouldHughdo*

Did you have any idea there was so much power in getting clarity on what you want?

But wait, there's one more important piece of the puzzle.

How do you feel?

Sometimes getting clarity on what you want, and focusing on it, is all you need to propel yourself forward. When clarity gives you a thrill of excitement, follow it! Do what sounds fun, because that's your autopilot guiding you! Really! It's that simple!

1. When you're excited, your brain is lit up!

Think about your face when you're worried or frustrated. In fact, go ahead and make that face. Do you feel how things scrunch up? Did you know that's happening inside your brain as well? Now make the face you make when you're excited and delighted. Everything expands and opens up. When that happens inside your brain, the blood flow increases and you are, quite literally, "firing on all cylinders."

This is the biggest problem with the "grit" concept that has been hot in the self-help market of late. If you push forward when something feels hard or you're frustrated or discouraged, you're not making decisions with your best brain. Sure, you can make things happen that way, but it's often much harder than it needs to be! When you insist on "work before play," you're likely to miss creative solutions or ideas that could save you heaps of time and frustration. The best productivity secret in the world is to prime your brain with positive expectation FIRST, then work.

2. What does feeling bad tell you?

Sometimes when you think about something you want, the primary emotion you feel is frustration that you don't have it, or that what you've tried so far is not working. Being really aware of your emotions is the second key piece of the Joy Revolution.

Before I go any farther, I want to be REALLY clear that the Joy Revolution is NOT about pretending everything is always joyful. It's about paying attention to how you feel and **understanding what your emotions are telling you**. *Ok? Are you with me on that?*

Because here's the good news. You don't have to wait until you're stuck in a snowbank to know where your autopilot is leading. Your emotions are your early detection system, kind of like those new-fangled cars that beep when you're veering out of your lane.

Have you ever played the hot-cold game? A child hides an object, then you look for it based on their directions. When you're moving closer to it that's "warmer," and when you're moving away from it, that's "colder." With those simple instructions, you will ALWAYS find what you're looking for. That, my friend, is the true game of life! That's the Joy Revolution in a nutshell. The more positive emotion you feel, the closer you are to your most optimized path.

Want the brain science behind that? Of course you do, because you're catching on to how much easier life is when you learn how to use your autopilot brain to your advantage!

Have you heard the expression "train of thought"? That's a great analogy because your thoughts are connected, and they build momentum. We're going to carry that analogy farther. Imagine something you want as an engine powering your train of thought forward. That's what internal motivation is.

So why are some people more motivated than others? Because not only do you have Want Engines, you also have Belief Engines. When you want something AND you have a strong belief that it's possible, even likely, you're unstoppable! Creative ideas flow and obstacles don't slow you down in the least. Both engines are powering in the same direction: forward! But what if you don't believe in yourself? That Belief Engine puts the brakes on, or even pulls in the opposite direction of your Want Engine.

Keep in mind that Belief Engines serve an evolutionary purpose. Fear is designed to warn you of danger. *Don't walk that way, there's a pack of hungry lions hiding!* Or to move forward a few thousand years, *Hmmm, I don't believe it's a good idea to walk down that dark street alone. I think I'll find another route or find another person to walk with me.* But when your Belief Engines are "protecting" you from positive changes, you can learn how to change their direction.

Imagine your Train of Thought with a strong Want Engine pulling forward and an equally strong Belief Engine pulling *backward*. What do you think that looks like in terms of emotion? You got it. Tension, frustration, building to anger, building to exhaustion and leading to giving up.

Being constantly frustrated or discouraged wears you out, so if you don't know about Belief Engines, the only option you have for finding relief from the tension is to slow down your Want Engine. You end up talking yourself out of your goals, or telling yourself to be content with what you have. The folks who teach "grit" have good intentions—they don't want you to give up on what you want! But that's missing an important piece.

A lot of motivational speakers try to rev up your Want Engine to just pull harder. But are you starting to see the picture of what that does inside your brain? Doesn't it make much more sense to slow down that non-Belief Engine so it's not pulling backward so hard, even get it turned around so it's moving forward? A lot of trainers and coaches are starting to emphasize the importance of believing in yourself. But *how* do you do that? What do you do when you don't?

3. How do you turn those engines around? HOW do you believe in yourself?

There are times when simply being aware of what your emotions tell you about your Belief Engines is enough to flip a switch and turn them around. You can stop and say to yourself:

> *Wait a minute. Do I believe what I want is possible? I don't have to believe it's a sure thing, just that it's possible. So I'm going to focus less on what could go wrong and focus more on what could go right!*

If you feel an emotional shift, a sense of relief, you've done it! You've turned the Belief Engine around and your autopilot is no longer pointed toward what you don't want, it's pointing toward what you do want!

Sometimes it's not that easy, if you've built up momentum around what could go wrong. One quick and easy thing to use to slow that momentum is a distraction to take the power away from it. I call these intentional distractions Joy Bringers. They can be different for everyone, but here are some ideas:

- Deep breaths
- Listen to a favorite song
- Stand up and stretch
- Dance break!
- Look out the window
- Pet your dog (or watch fish, any animal interaction)
- Take a walk

- Take a nap
- Call a friend
- Watch a cat video on YouTube (or a video of Hugh Jackman singing!)

#JoyRevolutionTip: Make a list of your favorite Joy Bringers on your phone, so when you need a quick uplift you can choose something from the menu.

Journaling is another tool. Did you know handwriting is a shortcut to reprogramming your autopilot brain? A simple prompt to start with for almost any situation is *The best possible outcome here is…*

Sometimes that Belief Engine comes in the form of a But. *I really want to try that new business, but I'm afraid I would fail.* "But" is a really powerful tool if you use it the right way. It takes the power out of whatever comes before it and puts more power in what comes after it. So when a But is slowing you down, simply **Flip the But**.

I know it could fail, but I really want to try that new business, because… (fill in the blank to give more momentum to what could go right!) The emotion is really different, isn't it? That simple tool can reduce the momentum of the backwards engine and increase your momentum forward.

4. *What about stubborn non-Belief engines?*

Sometimes you've had non-Belief engines pulling backward for a looooong time and they've built up quite a bit of power and momentum. When it seems especially hard to slow down a non-Belief engine, start by getting less specific with what you want. This will allow the backwards momentum to slow down, then you'll be able to gradually get more specific again with your Belief engine pointing forward.

The least specific you can get is to think about *how it will feel* when you get whatever you're focused on. Everything you want, you want it because of how you will feel when you have it (per Abraham Hicks). You want to feel successful, or attractive, or free, or safe, or relaxed, or connected. Once you've identified the desired feeling, write down any example you can come up with of how you *already have that feeling*.

If what you want is to be in better shape because you want to feel attractive, in what ways do you already feel attractive? (Yes, this might

18

take practice at first, but it will get easier.) Maybe you like your hair. Or your eyes. Maybe teal is a good color on you. Focus on those things until you can feel your emotion shift, that feeling of relief. (That change in emotion means your non-Belief engine is slowing its momentum.)

Another trick for persistent non-Belief engines is to understand the logical progression of emotions. Despair and fear are a long distance away from excitement and joy. That's why, when you're feeling really worried or discouraged, and some sunny person comes along telling you to "look on the bright side," you kind of want to kick them in the teeth.

There's much more detail about the Emotional Scale in books by either Dana Wilde or Esther Hicks, but here's the piece I use most often for myself and my team:

Fear --- Anger --- Frustration --- Hope

When you're stuck in fear or worry, the easiest way out is to intentionally get angry. Many of us grew up believing anger was always bad, but it can be a powerful tool. The key is not to get stuck there, but to move through it. A journal is a great tool once again. Start writing *I'm so angry that...* and keep writing until you've written everything you can come up with.

Next you'll soften your anger into frustration. Stand up and stretch or walk around, take a few deep breaths, then come back to your journal and start writing *It's just frustrating that...* A lot of the same things may come out, but the emotion will be less intense. That slowing of momentum will allow you to bridge to Hope.

Take a few more deep breaths and start writing again: *I really hope...*

The blood flow in your brain will be better and your Belief Engine will be starting to move in the right direction. You don't have to get to the place where you believe something is happening immediately, it's enough to believe something is possible. Then the momentum will build from there.

Hugh talks about dreams and dragons – a similar concept to Want Engines and Belief Engines. Isn't there power in knowing you don't necessarily need to 'slay' dragons, you can tame them! You can redirect them and use their power to move **toward** your dreams!

5. *Trust what brings you Joy.*

Really! The things that thrill you and light you up are truly what you are meant to do in the world! We have to unlearn some messages, such as that myth that success only comes from doing things you don't want to do. That is **not** the fastest path to making your mark. The simple truth is, when you are lit up, you light up the world around you. A friend of mine who loves hiking and camping used to joke that she wished someone would pay her to go hiking. When she started embracing the idea of doing what she loves, she created a business called Wander Women, where she plans hiking and camping excursions for people who aren't confident in the outdoors but want to experience it. She is getting paid to do exactly what she loves to do and is bringing joy and health to others!

When you get your autopilot focused on what you want, then life becomes a simple hot-cold game of asking, "Does that move me toward Joy?" Things that attract you point the way. When making decisions, I use this simple technique borrowed from *The Celestine Prophecy.*

1.   *Get a picture in your head of one option, then the other.*
2.   *Which mental picture was in brighter color? That's your choice!*

All you need to know is **#WIWHIF** – What I Want & How I Feel.

Let's review how this looks in daily life.

<u>When What You're Thinking About Feels Good</u>

- Feed it
- Build the momentum
- Share it
- Your autopilot is moving toward what you want, so brainstorm ideas and go with what sounds FUN!

When you feel successful, it's easy to keep going because that feeling builds momentum!

When What You're Thinking About Feels Bad

- Congratulate yourself on being aware of how you feel
  - (Beating yourself up is never productive. Never. It only gives momentum to what you don't want)
- Slow the momentum
  - Take some deep breaths
  - Play a song, take a walk, or other joy bringers
- State what you **do** want—what do you wish it looked like?
  - Get less specific or play around with descriptions until you feel a feeling of relief – that means your Belief Engine is shifting
- What's already going right?
  - What's going well that you can build on? (Hint: You can ALWAYS use that you're aware of how you're feeling and that's the first step!)
- When you can articulate what you want in a way that *at least feels hopeful*, THEN your autopilot is moving toward what you want, so brainstorm ideas and go with what sounds FUN!

The most common thing people do wrong is try to figure out what they're doing wrong! That strengthens your autopilot toward what you don't want! *Get your autopilot brain headed in the right direction, then move toward Joy.*

Are you getting excited about using this knowledge to live a more empowered, joyful life? With the power of clarity, and getting your Want Engines and Belief Engines powering forward together, you are going to change the world and have a BLAST doing it!

The Joy Revolution is not a switch you flip once, or a destination where you arrive and are finished. It's a lifelong journey. And there's no better way to see this journey in action than through the context of Hugh and Deb's story!

PART II
WHAT I LEARNED
FROM HUGH AND DEB

CHAPTER 3

BEFORE THEY WERE THEY

Deborra-lee Furness was born in November 1955 in a southern suburb of Sydney, Australia and moved to Melbourne shortly thereafter. Deb's dad died when she was very young, so she was raised by her amazing single mother, Fay. When Deb was five, Fay made the decision to enroll Deb in a convent boarding school near Daylesford, over 100 km away, since she wasn't able to care for her full time and earn a living. The separation was pretty hard on Fay, but Deb seemed to take it in stride.

Even when they weren't physically together every day, what Deb got in abundance from her mother was a strong sense of self-worth, a belief that she could do anything she set her mind to, and the confidence to always be herself. She basked in being the light of her mom's life, and was raised with a foundation of finding joy in being REAL. Well, except Deb had a lively imagination and didn't let the truth get in the way of a good story. In a class that she found boring, she told the teacher long, detailed stories about her miserable, neglected home life while her mother carried on a wild affair with Australian entertainer Graham Kennedy. It garnered her some leniency in grading until parent/teacher night when the teacher learned there was a quite a bit of fantasy involved in her tales.

But other than a storyteller's tendency to be creative, Deb believes "We are all the best when we are completely authentic." She wrote in a December 2017 column:

> *My mother taught me, by example, that you create your own reality, and everything is possible. She taught me that hurdles are jumpable and that as Muhammad Ali once*

quoted, "Impossible is not a fact." I hope I pass that on to my children and for them to pass it on to theirs.

Deb lived the Joy Revolution from the beginning.

Hugh Michael Jackman was born in October 1968 in a northern suburb of Sydney. He was the fifth child born in seven years to Chris and Grace, who moved from the UK to Australia while Grace was pregnant with their fourth baby.

At the time, Deborra-lee was approaching her 13th birthday, and that year her mother remarried. Deb attended many different schools, finishing at Methodist Ladies' College, a renowned boarding school. She started acting in plays at school, but it wasn't considered a "cool" thing to do. Her friends attended her performances, but it was mostly to give her a hard time! She hints that she may have occasionally skipped school to be a TV extra...

One friend said about her, "When I first met you as a teenager, I remember you had an incredible largess of spirit, and years have not flagged that." Deb recalls being the class clown, and when someone suggested she go into comedy, she was thrilled to learn you could actually get paid for making people laugh!

Deb has never been limited by the way things have always been done, a trait I adore and seek to emulate. In fact, I think she gets an extra thrill out of shaking things up. "I love going against what is expected."

For Hugh, the theater bug bit early – he played the King in his kindergarten class production of *Camelot*. Even though his too-large crown dropped down covering his face in mid-song, the greatest showman already had the stage presence to embrace the audience's laughter and keep singing!

Those lyrics provide such an interesting starting point for an exploration of Joy. The 1960s song talks of the ideal weather and precise seasons of Camelot, declaring it therefore an exemplary "happily-ever-aftering" spot.

We used to think of happiness as an emotional response to what was happening around us. So naturally a perfect happily-ever-after scenario would require perfect conditions. We've made such progress in understanding that regardless of our circumstances, we can connect with Joy and Dreams for what comes next. In 2017's The Greatest Showman, the impoverished tailor's son sings about falling asleep at night with his head full of exciting possibilities for the future.

Instead of happiness coming from good things, we now understand it's the other way around. Choosing to move toward happiness leads to good things.

The first movie Hugh remembers seeing was *The Wizard of Oz*. He was about five, and was completely drawn in by Dorothy's world. "If I Only Had a Brain" was his favorite song. But the flying monkeys were terrifying and he spent the last 15 minutes of the show under his chair crying. *I so relate to that experience! One of my own earliest memories was going to a puppet show of Peter Rabbit. All was going along fine with the rabbit and vegetable puppets dancing around. But Mr. McGregor was played by an actual person's legs walking around among the puppets. I was absolutely terrified and also found myself under the seat with my eyes shut tight until that part was over.*

Around the time of Hugh's elementary stage debut, Deb finished secretarial college and got a job at a TV news station. But she still loved acting, and at age 20, she landed her first minor TV role in *Division 4*, a police drama.

When Hugh was eight, his mother, suffering from a mix of postpartum depression and homesickness, abruptly left to return to England to care for her ailing mother. She said good-bye to the kids when they headed off to school as if it were a normal morning, but when they came home she was gone. Chris Jackman did his best caring for the five kids while working full time as an accountant. Hugh recalls that initially he hated walking into an empty house after school, so he would sit outside on the stoop waiting for one of his siblings to come home before going inside. For the most part, Chris ran the household without hired help after Grace left. But Hugh does remember acting a bit like the von Trapp children when his father hired a part-time nanny. Hugh and Ralph would stop at the butcher shop down the street on their way home from school and get cow eyes to leave in their lunchboxes for her to find. She didn't last very long. Sometimes Chris would pick up the kids from school and bring them back to the office while he finished his day of work.

"My mum's departure was a big, defining moment for me. It was terrible," Hugh reflected. "I couldn't quite understand it, and I kept thinking that she'd come back." His dad says Hugh has always been "remarkably mature for his age." My guess is that's related to having to grow up quickly when Grace left. And Hugh remembers being aware that in addition to the pressure of running the household, his father was heartbroken. Chris tried to for several years to reconcile the relationship.

As a pretty intense mom myself, it's hard to imagine being several continents away from my kids. But I know enough about Depletion Syndrome to imagine what Grace's life might have been like. Five pregnancies in seven years, a husband who traveled a lot for work, and living in a new hemisphere with the rest of her family thousands of miles away couldn't have been easy. And she was still pretty young, having been swept off her feet by Chris at a resort in Switzerland when she was only 19. Her leaving was abrupt to Hugh, but we don't know what conversations between Chris and Grace preceded it.

The simplest analogy is that Grace waited too long to put on her oxygen mask.

Although those years weren't easy, theater was a bright spot in Hugh's life. The first stage production he remembers seeing was *Man of La Mancha*. He was in fifth grade, and the play was at Knox Grammar School, his older brother's school where Hugh would later go also. The lead in that production was none other than Hugo Weaving, who would become best known for his role in *The Matrix*.

Hugh's dreams at this age were of travel. He had a map of the world on the wall next to his bed. He would look at the map and imagine being in Moscow and Greece and many different places. Those dreams have certainly come to fruition! It's dizzying to follow Hugh's travels when he's shooting or promoting a movie.

Another dream Hugh and his brother shared was to be in the *Guinness Book of World Records*. They tried to stay up all night playing badminton to set the record for the longest game, then they tried seeing how many coins they could flip off their elbows and catch. Sadly, they didn't reach their goal then. It didn't occur to Hugh to shoot for the record length playing a superhero character in movies! It was priceless to see the look on his face (in February 2019) when the editor-in-chief of the world record book told him he will be in the 2020 edition!

Dreams really do have power, sometimes in ways we least expect.

Watching the Oscars on television was memorable for the Jackman kids, but not for the reason you might expect. They would stand on the couch and cheer when the Price Waterhouse accountants came onstage with their briefcases (to give legitimacy to the calculating of results). Chris was an accountant for Price Waterhouse, and one year he recognized a man on stage as someone he'd met in a meeting! They figured that was the closest connection they'd ever have to the Academy Awards. 30-ish years later, Hugh would be the host.

Although a career in acting seems to be the polar opposite of accounting, Hugh has one key trait in common with his dad – he hates debt. However, a trait he chose not to emulate is that his dad used to buy fruit that was a little moldy or a little bruised, not because they couldn't afford better, but because he hated anything going to waste if the store was going to throw it out. Hugh continues to not like having excess stuff around, but he sure likes top quality food!

During this time, Deb was promoted to researcher at the TV station, and continued acting any chance she got. She started looking at options for more formal acting training. There were choices within Australia, and several of her friends were planning to study in London, but Deb was feeling a pull to New York. She took on a third job working the door at a nightclub to save more money in preparation.

What we think of as work ethic is people being fueled by powerful dreams.

In late elementary school, a teacher noticed Hugh's aptitude for dance and recommended he get lessons. Hugh was all for it until his older brother said it was a sissy thing to do, so he dropped the idea. He calls himself the "un-Billy-Elliot" story.

When Hugh was 12, his mother returned to try to reconcile. He was incredibly relieved, but unfortunately it only lasted a few weeks. When she left again, and Hugh's sisters went with her, his anger boiled over. It was a tough year at school. Teenage hormones added fuel to the frustration at home, and Hugh remembers swearing at teachers and having moments in rugby games where it felt like rage took over his body. He would draw on this pent-up frustration later to portray Wolverine.

Being the youngest with older brothers meant Hugh often got the short end of the stick in wrestling matches or brotherly fights. As the years pass, Hugh opens up more and more about the reality of those days. "My brother Ralph drove me nuts. I don't mind saying this publicly, but there were times when I thought, 'OK, I think I'm going to have to kill him, because if I just knock him out, he'll wake up and kill me.'" Recently he told an interviewer, "I was constantly fighting [with Ralph] and we were all living in chaos. Dad would come home late, usually not before seven at night, and there was always some trouble going on. It wasn't the best way to grow up."

Sometimes contrast is the best teacher. Hugh had a clear picture of what he did NOT want for his future family. That's one key to living a Joy-led life: being able to take a negative experience and translate it into a clear picture of what you DO want.

In what Deb calls "a huge leap of faith," she came to New York City at age 25 to study at the American Academy of Dramatic Arts. The pull of acting was that it seemed "fun and easy." *Joy Revolution, straight up.* What did her mum think? "I don't think she was overly thrilled, but she allowed me to follow my bliss, to follow MY dream to do that, and I'm so grateful for her," Deb said. How did Deb feel? "It was amazing. It was life changing," she says of her time studying there. She not only fell further in love with acting, she fell in love with the city. Deb has said, "I feel like my kid grew up as this chubby little curly-haired girl from Melbourne. But my adult is a sassy New Yorker." And on the practical side, she earned income by working as a telephone pollster, which she used as an opportunity to do her dialect homework—practicing different American accents!

Meanwhile, Hugh finished elementary school and entered Knox, a private all boys' school. (Figuring it was his last chance for a long time, he did finagle a way to kiss a girl once before moving up!) Knox was a Presbyterian Scottish school by tradition, so their uniforms included kilts for certain occasions. Not Hugh's favorite. "Years of being made fun of! Can you imagine in Australia you have to catch the bus to school and you're wearing a skirt?"

At age 13, Hugh had a strong premonition about his future career. Watching the preacher at a revival meeting, he had a sense he'd be up on stage like that someday, in front of a crowd. At the time, he assumed that meant he would be a minister. On one occasion he even had the chance to preach a sermon at the school chapel. (He doesn't remember what he said. Aren't you curious??) He also dreamed of being a professional rugby player. Or a rock star.

Since the Greatest Showman soundtrack album was the top selling album IN THE WORLD in 2018 and won a Grammy, I'd say that dream has come true! And with the world tour this year, definitely put a big old check mark next to rock star on the vision board!

30

The next year, about the time Deb graduated from AADA, Hugh's pal Gus convinced him to try out for the school musical, *The Music Man*, because it was being done in partnership with a local girls' school. An over-achiever even then, Hugh learned all eight parts of the traveling salesmen's opening scene for the audition (and learned it well enough that he remembers it to this day!) Hugh continued his school theatre adventures (was it just about the girls, or was it a growing love of the stage?) starring as Tommy in *Brigadoon* and as Henry Higgins in *My Fair Lady*. The students at Knox were also encouraged to put on their own plays, which he loved.

Music was a consistent thread in his education. I'm not sure to what extent he studied each, but he played violin, piano, and guitar. Although his brother had talked him out of taking dance classes, he put those long legs to good use competing in the high jump and playing cricket and rugby. Hugh loved the intensity of rugby. "If there wasn't blood coming from somewhere on my body, I was disappointed that I hadn't played hard enough." Then he would go home, shower, and flop on the couch to watch old musicals for the afternoon. You'll find him in the dictionary under "well-rounded." And yes, his love of theater was about more than just working with the neighboring girls' school. For his 18th birthday, he asked for a season ticket to the Sydney Theatre Company. Those Saturday matinees were a highlight of each month.

His likability and charisma were already in full evidence, and he was chosen captain of the school in his final year. And he did come full circle regarding dance. Ralph and Hugh and their dad went to see *42nd Street*. At intermission Ralph apologized to Hugh for having previously talked him out of dancing and said he belonged onstage. Hugh hadn't thought about it that much in the meantime, but realized that yes, he would enjoy it! So he signed up for a tap class the very next day. Tap dancing is still one of Hugh's favorite forms of exercise. Does he regret possibly missing out on a career as a professional dancer? No, *Hugh doesn't really look backward*. He believes he's exactly where he is meant to be in life.

That's a powerful Joy Revolution tip. Don't spend time fretting over what you can't change anyway. Start where you are. Always. Look back only to remind you how far you've come, otherwise focus forward.

He brought his trademark friendliness to his job as a cashier at a gas station. A woman who grew up in that area recalls that she had previously run out of gas several times, but during the time Hugh worked at the station, she developed the habit of filling up much more regularly. *She had*

31

her own little Joy Revolution experience! See how things that bring us joy can help us develop good habits? ☺ But with charm can come heartache as well. "I remember getting dumped when I was 15. It was the end of the world. 'I will never love again. This is a disaster.'" One instance of how looking back has changed how Hugh moves forward is that he realizes now it would have been ok to have taken school a little less seriously and had a little more fun! So he now lives with that in mind.

A little less nose-to-the-grindstone, a little more Joy. How many people wait to come to that realization until they're at the very end of their life?

Hugh was in secondary school, and Deb was a busy, thriving actress. After finishing at AADA in 1982, Deb intended to stay and work in the US, but returned to Australia for the holidays first. She fit in as many auditions as she could while she was home, just for practice. But she quickly started getting offers, including the TV show, *Kings*, and a guest role on the first year of the soap opera, *Neighbors*. Roles on *Glass Babies* and *The Flying Doctors* followed, and more offers, both in movies and on television. Wanting to share her love of acting with others, she and a friend founded D.A.G. Productions and offered acting classes. The name stood for Deb And Greg but they also enjoyed the play on the Australian slang word for a quirky but likeable person.

But then, in late 1985, Deb was in a serious car accident. Multiple broken bones and bad cuts on her face led her to believe her acting career was over. However, a casting agent who had read the script of *Shame* believed Deb was perfect for that role and convinced her, even before she got out of the hospital, to audition.

Did the physical and emotional experience of that accident give Deb a new level of range and power that propelled her to stardom in Shame? Think of the analogy of a caterpillar in a cocoon – those moments when we think life as we know it is over, we're transforming. That's how I was in the middle of my traumatic divorce. I didn't know how I would go on living, but it was actually the beginning of the journey toward becoming fully ME. What if, even when you're smack in the middle of those experiences, you could see the end of the story? What if you could picture yourself telling Oprah about it, how those dark times opened you up to see new possibilities and led to the best parts of your life?

After graduating in 1986, Hugh was chosen as one of two students from his class to spend six months as a teaching assistant at Uppingham School in London. His duties ranged from teaching physical education to tutoring younger students in English and drama. A former student didn't spill too many details on what he was like as a teacher, but remembered him as being tall and skinny, and that the students all assumed he was around age 24. He must have exuded an air of authority! After his time teaching, he and friends backpacked around Europe, sometimes sleeping on the train to save money. It was during that year, at age 18, that he saw snow for the first time.

While Hugh was in Europe, Deb landed the lead role in *Shame* and filming began in Western Australia. Her fiery, gutsy performance as the motorcycle-riding, leather-wearing young attorney, Asta, won her several awards and a new level of international fame including the milestone of having her face on a billboard in Times Square. The studio didn't tell her ahead of time about the billboard, just drove her by and said, "Look up there!" When Deb shared that exciting news with her mum, Fay told her to be sure and take a picture, but Deb didn't have a camera. "Buy one!" Fay said.

That little story is such a great example of Fay's influence. She went for an immediate, obvious solution to the problem of not having a camera at that important moment. You get the sense she was confident Deb would have a lot more occasions she would want to capture on film.

A *New York Times* reporter writing about the movie asked Deb if she considered herself a feminist. Deb replied with her trademark light-hearted but candid style: "I believe in equal rights, if that's what it is. I also believe in shaving my legs." Promoting *Shame*, sometimes girls would come up and thank Deb for telling their story. That's when she realized "through my work I can really affect people." Deb said, "She was my favorite character I ever played probably because like me she was a justice freak."

Through doing what sounded fun and easy to her, Deb found her vehicle to impact the world.

Promoting *Shame* in America renewed her intention to act in the US, and provided the connections to make it happen! Deb was one of the pioneering Australians in the US acting market. Her first American role was on the TV series *Falcon Crest*. In fact, she admits she had quite a crush on Lorenzo Lamas, who played Lance. (Since Lamas recently divorced his fifth wife, I think Deb did well to keep her distance.) *Act of Betrayal* with co-star Elliott Gould followed. It wasn't an easy road, though, for an

Australian doing auditions in the US. Directors weren't used to their accent. Deb was advised to use an American accent from the moment she introduced herself, but that felt fake to her, and we know how much she values authenticity. Deb auditioned for the role of Stands With a Fist in *Dances With Wolves.* They really liked her work on camera but were nervous about casting an Australian.

While Deb was going back and forth working in both Australia and the US, Hugh had enrolled at the University of Technology Sydney, aiming for a career in journalism. He describes himself as an "average student" doing what he needed to do to get by. Clearly he hadn't yet found his mission in life. His Investigative Journalism teacher was Wendy Bacon, a well-known Australian journalist and activist, and he remembers thinking he didn't have half the passion she had for the subject. He performed in student and community theater productions for fun.

A classmate recommended Hugh consider modeling, so he had some photos taken but was rejected by the agency he applied to. Looking back now that agent tells Hugh that turning him down as a model was the best thing he could have ever done for him. Yes, Hugh is lovely to look at, but we're glad he has shared his broader gifts!

Hugh spent one summer working in an Aboriginal community in Central Australia. Originally building homes as part of a mission, he then said he'd "have a go" at managing a local general store so the owner could have some time off. "The locals loved it because I'm sure they were nicking so much stuff, and I had no idea," he said. Or maybe they found him as irresistible and uplifting as the rest of us do and simply enjoyed his presence at the center of their community.

This time in the outback is when he first started to contemplate who he was and who he wanted to be in the world. "There was enough quiet in my head, I suppose, for me to get an inkling of who I was." Wow. That statement is worth reading again. He loved the feeling of peace in the Aboriginal culture so much, he called his dad and said he was considering staying there instead of returning to Sydney. His wise father encouraged him to complete his degree first, then go back west afterward if he still wanted to. He went back to the university, but the groundwork was laid. That depth of introspection and spirituality has continued throughout his life.

At our core, we are drawn toward Joy. And when our minds are quiet, we start dreaming.

His final year at UTS included a class in journalism ethics. Hugh had been very idealistic about the job, but through studying ethical dilemmas he realized there would be a lot of messy, complicated days in that career. Fate crooked its finger at him when he took an acting class for two "easy" credits. Roles in the class production were assigned alphabetically according to each character's appearance, so the luck of the draw gave Hugh the lead. He made a desperate plea to the professor to get out of it due to his thesis workload, but there was no sympathy. (The play was Vaclav Havel's *The Memorandum*, for you theater buffs.)

As it happened, it was the most fun he ever had in a class, and he started to consider if acting really could be more than a hobby. He recalls thinking during that class, "Hmm, I'm spending about an hour a day on my thesis and about 15 hours a day on this play — have I made the wrong choice?" His class visited an acting class at another university to perform the play and were hosted overnight by students there. As Hugh got to know the group in the house where he stayed, he had a flash of clarity. "'These are my people.' You just know. 'This is my tribe.'"

That's such a good point, isn't it? The people with whom you feel most at home, with whom you feel most completely yourself, are a great barometer for you to know you've found your path.

I can relate to this with my own college experience. I started as a math education major, with a minor in music. But the way I connected with my fellow students in music theory, orchestra, and choir, vs. how I felt with my fellow math students... Well, there was no comparison. I got there gradually – bumped up to a double major, then my third year realized I didn't give a rat's ass about advanced calculus and finished with just one degree, in music. Practical? Not at all. Do I regret spending that time focusing on what was lighting me up? Not a bit. I found a job with an insurance company that was looking for people who could think and communicate. The specific area of study didn't matter to them. Of course I'm still not totally sure, at 47, what I want to be when I grow up. What I'm sure of is that I want to enjoy life.

While Hugh was at UTS, Deb's career continued to expand. In *The Last of the Finest,* she played the wife of actor Brian Dennehy. Since he was a pretty big guy, Deb sweetly asked the director if she could be on top during their love scene! She also won the role of Ivy in the movie *Voyager*, where she had a very steamy shower scene with Sam Shepard. Deb asked one of the more experienced actresses on set if she should be concerned about her co-star becoming aroused while filming a scene like that. "I'd be offended if he didn't," was the older woman's response. While Deb was in LA, fellow Aussie Nicole Kidman came to the US to try her hand in Hollywood and slept on Deb's couch. One of Nicole's auditions was for *Days of Thunder.* Deb remembers at one point saying in a heated whisper, "Nicole! Tom Cruise is on the phone!"

Hugh completed his communications degree in November 1990. Then while sorting out what he wanted to do next, he took a job working the front desk at a gym (the way he tells it he was the skinny kid processing paperwork who got teased by the personal trainers), and auditioned for a part-time course called The Journey at the Actors' Centre in Sydney. He got in (evidently just barely), but then found out the cost was $3500. Since he had just finished one degree, he felt he couldn't ask his dad for the money, so he threw away his acceptance letter. The very next day Hugh received a check for $3500 from his grandmother's estate.

Do you think the universe was lined up with Hugh's dream of acting?

The drama program didn't start off well. "For the first six months I was definitely the dunce of the class. Everything I did, like getting up for an improv, was met with an eye roll. It devastated me. I felt very alienated and powerless. It only turned around when I thought, 'Stuff this, let's just have some fun.'" He reflected later, "I really have to thank all the staff at ACA for instilling in me that sense of play, risk taking and adventure that has made acting so fulfilling for me."

Hugh's Joy Revolution had begun.

A good signal that Hugh had found his path was how he was going way above and beyond what was expected. They were given an assignment to watch one of the John Barton *How to Play Shakespeare* tapes. Hugh was so enamored he spent hours in the library watching all the tapes. A dream took shape of someday being part of the Royal Shakespeare Company.

As Hugh was learning to let go and trust what felt fun as an acting student, Deb continued kicking up her heels in Hollywood, including playing the role of Esther Jacobs in *Newsies,* Disney's first completely live-action movie musical. Continuing to hop back and forth across the pond, Deb appeared in the Australian movie *Angel Baby* and several TV roles, including *Halifax, F.P.* playing a cop who gets kidnapped by a serial killer. Jacqueline McKenzie, a co-star in *Angel Baby,* describes Deb's popularity.

Men loved Deborra-lee. The flowers that arrived! We were working in the desert where it's hard to get fresh-cut flowers but by god they used to come in by the truckload going straight up the stairs into her trailer. And she wouldn't lead anyone on at all, she's just genuinely a very beautiful person that you want to either be or be around.

(Fun fact: Jacqueline was in the production of *Brigadoon* with Hugh in high school! While she was working with Deb, could she have imagined that the guy she and her friends had drooled over in school would be the one who would capture Deb's heart forever?)

Back in Sydney, one day a woman Hugh was enrolling at the gym suddenly looked closely at him and gasped. She said she was a white witch (someone who uses her powers for good) and that he had to go into acting, that he was going to be a big star. At first he thought, "Please, just give me your credit card" to finish the enrollment process, but then realized he had nothing to lose by listening. She was Annie Semler, wife of cinematographer Dean Semler. She introduced him the next day to Penny Williams, who became his first agent.

Penny arranged an audition with the popular Australian soap opera *Neighbors,* and Hugh was offered a role with a two year contract and a starting salary of $2000 a week. (I'm not surprised, are you?) His younger sister in London was probably the most excited, telling all her friends about her brother's upcoming role, which made her very popular at school!

However, many students in Hugh's class at the Actors Centre had been talking about the amazing acting school at the Western Australian Academy for the Performing Arts (WAAPA) in Perth. Hugh thought about his ultimate dream to do Shakespeare on London's West End, and asked himself which would move him closer to that dream – *Neighbors* or WAAPA. The answer in his heart was he wanted more training and confidence as an actor. That was reinforced by their dad drumming into them that education is always a good investment. However, *Neighbors* wanted an answer only a few days after Hugh's WAAPA audition. So at the end of his audition, he approached the panel and said he didn't want to be presumptuous, but he had this job offer that needed a decision and could they give him an idea if they thought he'd be accepted or not? WAAPA called the next morning and offered him a spot in their program, so Hugh had a decision to make. After wavering back and forth that weekend, he turned down the *Neighbors* gig. It took his little sister a long time to forgive him.

Sometimes decisions can seem hard when you're focused on the immediate impact or on what's practical in the moment, but when you keep your dreams in focus, you can safely follow your heart.

There were friends who thought he was nuts to turn down the job. Actors such as Russell Crowe and Chris Hemsworth got their starts on *Neighbors,* so I can see why people thought this was Hugh's big break. But Hugh could see bigger dreams, and he set aside conventional opportunities to follow those dreams. You see what I mean about *The Greatest Showman* being more Hugh Jackman than P.T. Barnum?

So how was the WAAPA experience? It was quite an adjustment. "I've never felt so fulfilled and so challenged, so depressed, so happy, so shucked around, so taken off my center, so no-longer-the-school-captain-who-will-always-land-on-his-feet, so lonely." But it turns out that opened him up to living in the moment, to allowing a full range of emotion. "For me it was an opportunity to find out what's underneath all that very presentable side of Hugh Jackman. Those three years are when I grew up."

Kind of makes you want to go to acting school, doesn't it?

This is a good time for a reminder that the Joy Revolution doesn't mean every moment is joyful. It's about having clear dreams and listening to your emotions. When you're expanding your comfort zone, you encounter new challenges. But when you have a dream in view, you can see bumps in the road as opportunities to clarify what you want and grow into a new version of yourself.

During his first year at WAAPA, while visiting his mum in London, Hugh got a photo of himself in front of one of the Royal National Theatre buildings, in a prayer position. That was his ultimate dream as an actor. He put that picture up on his wall at school.

Nice use of a vision board before they were cool.

Another key piece of Hugh's Joy Revolution journey happened during that time but wasn't a formal part of school. He noticed one of his fellow students had a general air of calm and optimism, and asked what his secret was. His friend introduced him to the School of Practical Philosophy. Meditation was a part of the course, which Hugh says "changed my life." I'll talk more about meditation and its role in my own Joy journey in chapter 11.

During his time at WAAPA Hugh earned money washing dishes at a restaurant. In a later interview, he told Martha Stewart he loved his time as a dishwasher, especially the rush from 8:30-10:30 at night. This guy likes INTENSITY. *For most of us that doesn't sound like fun at all, but that's an important point about the Joy Revolution. You get to decide for yourself what gets your blood flowing. And the more you can find joy in a variety of situations, the happier and healthier you will be.* Another perk of that job was the opportunity to eat leftovers from the plates that were brought to him to wash. (He didn't admit that little habit to Deb until 20-ish years later!)

Hugh loved the variety offered by WAAPA's program. "When I trained at acting school, you do fencing, Shakespeare class, modern dance, circus school, all before lunch." So for someone like him, the range of playing Wolverine, the regal Leopold, the sinister Blackbeard, and flamboyant Peter Allen was easy!

*I don't want to sound like a broken record, but it's such an important point that you get to decide what YOU love. For some people, constantly trying new things is exhausting, for others it's exhilarating. There's a danger in reading a book about Hugh and Deb that you'll start to feel like a second-rate lazy ass. ☺ I know I did writing it! The point is for you to find things in life that give you the same kind of **feeling** Hugh gets from acting. That's your sweet spot.*

When you're doing what you love, it's so much easier to be all in. Hugh never missed a day of classes at WAAPA, and he says the same was NOT true of his time at UTS... His senior year in movement class, they were given the assignment to recreate a famous scene, and Hugh chose the sword fight from *The Princess Bride*. I'm putting it on my manifesting list to see a video of that someday!

Going back to what we think of as work ethic, many directors have described Hugh as the "hardest-working actor in Hollywood." But no one ever described him as the hardest-working journalism student at UTS. When you're doing what you love, the fire that drives you is potent. In contrast, burnout, stress-related health issues, and addiction can all be by-products of forcing yourself to do things you don't really enjoy. Plus you would be depriving the world of your best you!

Hugh's WAAPA experience wrapped up with playing the lead in a production of *Romeo and Juliet*. His fellow students said never to give him a cameo role because he would steal the show. (Ahem. *X-Men First Class*.) "Do I? That sounds terrible doesn't it?" Hugh responded. Kudos to his parents for raising him with politeness to balance his charisma, but isn't it powerful to see someone so natural in their chosen field they can't help but shine?

Chris Jackman got to travel to Perth to see Hugh playing Romeo. The production was staged with the house lights up so the actors could interact with the audience. In one particularly emotional part of the story, Hugh caught sight of his dad crying. Chris was reflecting on the contrast between the hard times in Hugh's life, and how amazing it was to see his youngest son in his element. I can relate to that feeling as I watch my daughter perform in her circus arts showcases. Her favorite apparatus is aerial silks. There's an intense level of joy as a parent watching your child excel in what it feels like they were born to do.

As a matter of routine, the Australian Broadcasting Corporation is required to send a casting agent to all acting schools each year to give the students experience auditioning. The audition day that year was in the middle of the *Romeo and Juliet* run, so Hugh's focus was on Shakespeare. He figured the audition was just a routine box ABC had to check, so he performed the prisoner scene he'd been given, but had no nerves or stress about the process. A week later, Hugh found out he was at the top of the short list for an upcoming prison drama! They said the final audition would take place the night of his graduation showcase in Melbourne four weeks later. But on showcase day, they decided they didn't need to see him audition again and offered him the part!

How many actors land a starring role in a TV series the night they graduate from acting school? The director had loved Hugh's *relaxed* performance on his audition tape!

Your brain functions best when you're relaxed and happy.

Hugh received the Leslie Anderson Award for Most Outstanding Graduate of his class. Drama teacher Chris Edmund said, "He has that rare ability to make an audience of five or 12,000 feel included and to have experienced something special in his presence."

When you do what you love, you light up the world.

As graduation approached, Hugh's mate Gus Worland was preparing to get married in the UK. Hugh would have loved to attend the wedding, but funds were too tight, so instead he accepted his first paying gig as an actor – to spend one week filming an episode of *Law of the Land*. Hugh grimaces at the footage of him playing Aussie rules football, since he had been a rugby player, but he showed some pretty good acting chops, and already had the same ability to steal the show on screen that he did on stage. That first role included his first shirtless scene, and many of his roles since have followed suit, for which he takes a lot of ribbing (pun intended).

Deborra-lee had gone to see a fortune teller in Los Angeles, who told her she needed to go back to Australia, where she would find more professional success and meet the man of her dreams. Since she'd just experienced a string of auditions and rejections in the US, Deb figured there was nothing to lose so decided to follow that advice. She told her friend Mark Pennell she wanted to room with him, but she would only sign a year lease, because she would "be married within a year." Then she made a New Year's resolution to only date men over 30, and no actors. Presumably she was planning to find a good, solid, "regular" guy to settle down with.

The universe looked on with glee, knowing what was about to come together...

CHAPTER 4

THE STARS ALIGN

You know you're on the right path when things fall into place, like Hugh landing his first leading role on the very night of his graduation – playing the young heartthrob prisoner Kevin Jones opposite leading lady Deborra-lee Furness in the TV series *Corelli*. There was no screen test for chemistry in the audition process, so Hugh and Deb wouldn't meet until filming started.

But his agent wasn't satisfied with him landing one role, she clearly saw his potential in many areas. So even before *Corelli* started filming, she sent him to audition for the musical *Beauty and the Beast*. Hugh thought she was a little crazy, because while he had done musical theater in high school, he hadn't concentrated on it at WAAPA. He read the speaking part first and could tell the panel was excited about his performance. Then he sang Stars from *Les Mis*, and his voice cracked dramatically on the last note. The musical director told him to put that song away, he'd never be in that show. (I hope that guy saw his Oscar-nominated performance of Jean Valjean 17 years later.) Hugh said, "I didn't feel the pressure of the audition because I didn't think I had a chance of getting the role. Gaston is rather arrogant, yet comical at the same time, so I played it to the fullest in my audition—you have to love to hate him." The panel loved his charisma and stage presence so selected him for the role, but sent him to get some singing lessons.

Do you see a pattern already? Two auditions completed without worry or pressure, two breakout roles landed.

In January 1995 Hugh moved to a rented apartment on Beaconsfield Parade in Melbourne, ready to start his full-time acting career, excited to work with an actress he and many drama school buddies admired. (Several friends begged to visit him on set for a chance to meet Deb!) At that point Hugh had not seen *Shame* and he said it's probably a good thing he hadn't, or he would have been too intimidated to interact much outside of filming!

Hugh loves telling the story of the morning he and Deb first met. He went out to the car where the assistant director was picking them up for the first day, and Deb was already in the front seat. She turned around up on her knees, took off her sunglasses, and held out her hand, introducing herself with a big smile. Normal behavior for fun-loving, outgoing Deborra-lee, but Hugh hadn't expected that kind of warmth from a star. He was instantly charmed.

Though Deb initially couldn't get Hugh's name right (she called him Jack Human), her recollection is that acting with him was "thrilling," like "a great tennis match," or like finding someone you can dance well with. "We just knew how to move together," she said. "We laughed uproariously together, sometimes during the scene which wasn't always appropriate, but there was an amazing chemistry." Hugh agreed. "It was the best experience I've ever had working with another actor. This was before we were romantically involved or I had any idea that Deb was interested. There was a chemistry and a play, and every time we had a scene together it was unbelievable. Professionally I've never had anything quite like that again."

Watching them on screen together truly is magical. My favorite scene in the series is in episode 2, the moment Kevin decides to trust Louisa, drops his brain-damaged cover, and speaks as himself. It's electric. It's a remarkable talent for two actors to convey nonverbal soul to soul communication on camera. The producers said they were "very happy with the chemistry" between their two stars. I bet!

On a personal level, Deb recalls that from the beginning they were great friends – she would invite him to her place on weekends to rehearse their scenes – but initially she was so focused on learning lines, romance was the farthest thing from her mind. As she tells it, "[The prisoners] grunted at me, I had all the dialogue!" Plus, there had been that New Year's resolution not to date actors or anyone under 30. Then she started to notice that on days 26-year-old Hugh wasn't in scenes with her, she missed his presence...

The day Hugh realized he had a serious crush on his leading lady (through watching another actor fawn over her and realizing he was jealous), he was mortified. I don't know if it was explicitly taught in acting school, or just an unspoken industry rule, that off-screen romance kills on-screen chemistry, but Hugh felt ridiculous being such a cliché. After having been good friends for about six weeks, he cold-turkey stopped talking to Deb at all between scenes. He came to his senses after a few days and realized that wasn't a good long-term plan, so he decided to host a dinner party, inviting Deb and a bunch of other people.

Handheld cell phones were still somewhat rare in 1995, but Deborra-lee had one. And she kept it at her side at all times, including during dinner at Hugh's house. About halfway through the meal, it rang. It was a friend outside Hugh's place in a limo with Mick Jagger (!) asking Deb to come join them for the rest of the evening! When Deb declined because she was "hanging out with Hugh Jackman," Hugh (rightly) took that as a promising sign. He asked Deb if she would help him serve the dessert.

It wasn't just any dessert. Hugh's dad, an excellent cook, had suggested that a good way to impress guests was with Crepes Suzette. The bonus in this case was it required about an hour of prep time, giving Deb and Hugh some time alone—with the added benefit of a little alcohol in their systems.

Deb, not one for beating around the bush, came right out and asked why Hugh hadn't been talking to her recently. Hugh admitted his crush, adding, "I'm sorry, I'll get over it," nervously not looking at her as he spoke. She made a noncommittal noise which made Hugh's heart sink, then said, "Yeah, I have a crush on you, too." At first Hugh was too shocked to believe it, but I bet it sank in pretty quickly. Deb's roommate, Mark, who had accompanied her to the party, said he kept seeing her go back and forth taking plates to the kitchen so he finally decided to go see if he could help. He was quite surprised to find Hugh and Deb in a passionate embrace! Only two people know the whole story of the rest of that night, and neither of them is authoring this book. In one interview, Hugh said they never made it back to the table, but I have to assume he was kidding, as he's far too well-mannered to ditch a party he was hosting! (I think...)

What we do know is they tried to keep their relationship a secret on set for a few weeks. But they later found out their colleagues could see it written on Hugh's face every time he looked at Deb. Or maybe it was when an assistant director went to pick up Deb at 5:00 one morning and Hugh hopped in the car as well. Or maybe it was when the caterer walked in on them making out in Deb's dressing room. Or maybe it was when they thought they were alone and were talking about their evening plans, then

45

looked up and realized the boom microphones above them were live. There were some big eyes in the sound booth! (I'm guessing they were talking about more than where to eat dinner... Was this one of those "leave those tattoos on tonight" moments?) About three weeks in, Deb tried to break it off, going back to her earlier resolution not to date actors anymore. Hugh says "I managed to talk her around, thank God." Shortly thereafter, Hugh won the approval of Deb's girlfriends (a very important test), and Deb introduced him to her mother. Hugh did the dishes that first evening at Fay's house. Smart move.

As Hugh and Deb's off-screen relationship developed, on-screen Kevin and Louisa locked horns. It's so fun watching Kevin's fiery anger and Louisa's calm demeanor, knowing the actors' personalities are the reverse. Deb is the fiery rule-breaker and Hugh is the rational, even-tempered one. When they do finally lock lips in episode ten, it's intense. Hugh said they may have "overdone" it because they were worried people would think they'd "lost their edge" on screen, since he had "basically moved in" by then. Whatever their motivation, we – the viewers – are the beneficiaries.

But by the end of that episode—which would be the end of the series since *Corelli* didn't get picked up for a second season—our hearts are broken as they're separated for the remainder of Kevin's long sentence. I would hardly be able to watch it if I didn't know Hugh and Deb had their own happy ending. I relate to the supermarket checkout woman who saw them together after the series ended and said, "I knew it! I knew it was too good to be acting!"

Was their age difference an issue? Hugh's dad was concerned initially because of the absence of a mother in Hugh's daily life. "Is this a maternal thing?" he asked. Hugh just laughed. "I am literally the adult in this relationship," he said. "People always think I'm older than her because she's a lot more fun and bubbly and energetic than I am."

Stepping away from their story for a minute, it's serendipitous that the language I use to describe how to live the Joy Revolution – the What I Want & How I Feel system—came straight from Kevin Jones, hardened criminal. Since I happen to share the name of Deb's character, he was speaking directly to me.

> *In episode 4: "Forget the rules, Louisa. What do you want?"*
> *In episode 10: "Tell me how you feel, Louisa."*

So there you have it, Guru Kevin Jones explains brain science, decoding emotions, and the process of manifesting.

After *Corelli* wrapped, Hugh filmed one episode of the award-winning TV series *Blue Heelers*. There wasn't a lot of intense acting required, but when looking for someone to play a handsome, charming big city attorney, I can see why you'd cast Hugh. Actor John Wood recalls that Deb was on set also. "She seemed to be, in a sense, mentoring him." Sharing the art they have in common has been part of their entire relationship. "We're very involved in each other's creative lives," Deb said. They still read lines together preparing for roles.

As if there wasn't enough going on, Hugh also guest-starred in five episodes of *Snowy River: The McGregor Saga* which would air in the spring of 1996. His charm lit up the screen. Almost 20 years later, an interviewer was talking about people who get tattoos of Wolverine, and Hugh joked that he was surprised no one chose his character from *Snowy River* to get inked on their skin. I'd say Duncan would be a pretty damn cute choice to carry with you for life! One line in the show particularly made me smile, knowing Hugh's interests. A young woman who is enamored with Duncan (Hugh) said to him, "I'm talking about something important – us – and you prefer coffee."

Then Hugh went straight into rehearsals for *Beauty and the Beast*, which opened on July 8, 1995 in Melbourne. Not only did he prove his singing chops, he "set hearts a-flutter in every performance" according to one reviewer, and "stole the show," according to director Richard Wherrett. He's a "sexy, charismatic, charming performer, but more to the point I think he's got a depth in his talent." He also learned some important lessons about hydration during that show, but more on that later...

As a new star, he needed a little practice at media interviews. He tended to give long, rambling answers. (I sympathize—in my brief stint as a political candidate, I learned that 30-second sound bytes are not my forte.) But critics loved him. "Hugh Jackman may not yet be a national icon, but he is likely to attract attention in his role as the strapping braggard, Gaston." And his co-star Rachel still includes in her bio that she got kissed by Hugh Jackman and got paid for it. How did Hugh feel about it all? "I am living my boyhood dream as a member of the *Beauty and the Beast* cast. I just love it and have fun on stage in every show."

Joy. Fun. Dreams. Imagine if he had stuck to journalism, how the world would have missed out.

Hugh says he's not usually a decisive person but he knew with 100% confidence, after just two weeks of dating Deb, that she was the one. "When I met Deb, I knew immediately I was going to marry her. I forced myself to wait six months because I thought, 'Maybe it is infatuation. I'm too young to know.' It was ridiculous. Every day love just got deeper." How did he know? "I felt a complete trust with her to be exactly who I am. I don't have to be any other version of Hugh Jackman for her to love me."

That's pure relationship gold right there. A lesson for anyone considering making a relationship permanent – does it pass that test? I'll delve deeper into their amazing marriage in chapter 12.

So on September 5, 1995, at the Botanical Gardens in Melbourne, Hugh set a memorable stage. He arranged to have a table with breakfast and flowers set up near a lake, then asked Deb to join him in a casual morning walk. When they came around the bend to see the prepared scene, Deb initially assumed it must be a magazine photo shoot, but then Hugh said, "Surprise!" Deb exclaimed that it was "perfect." Quick on his feet, Hugh scrapped his carefully planned speech and said, "Well... it will be if you marry me!" Then he pulled out the ring he had designed himself. 20 years later when a reporter asked about the proposal, Hugh said, "I'm an actor, prone to exaggeration, so I was determined that was one story I wouldn't have to exaggerate. Did I do all right?" Of course Deb gushed about his flair for romance.

What made Deb change her mind after a resolution to stay away from young actors? "It was like he was my soulmate. It was someone I recognized." Deb's mother's reaction included a condition that surprised him! Fay told the story in a blog post:

> *When my daughter and Hugh fell in love, Hugh said to me,
> 'I've just proposed to Deborra-lee and I'd like your blessing.'
> I think he thought I'd go, 'Yay!' and, on the inside, I did, but
> I made him sit down. 'This is my daughter you're marrying
> and you have to look after her,' I said. I made him promise
> to love her forever, never go to bed on an argument, and
> that he had to be a patron of the Fight Cancer Foundation.*

He readily agreed.

Hugh was performing in a hit show on stage, and Deb was back on TV in *Fire*. But they found time to have a beautiful wedding on April 11, 1996. Adorably, the hard-working actor forgot his lines that day. He said as he started his vows, "I just went blank." Deb had his back, as she has from that day forward. Their first dance was to "All the Way" sung by Tom Burlinson and Kate Ceberano.

> *Who knows where the road will lead us*
> *Only a fool would say*
> *But if you'll let me love you*
> *It's for sure I'm gonna love you all the way*

Deb says it was the "best wedding I ever went to!"

Hugh's delightfully warped sense of humor was on display at the 2014 Empire Awards, in his Icon Award acceptance speech. Referring to the montage *Empire* had put together reviewing his career up to that point, he called it "a minute and a half of action, very little dialogue – kind of reminds me of my wedding night." Whatever, Hugh.

Hugh reflects that he's grateful he and Deb met before anything big happened in his career. They were "set, together, a team, madly in love" through all the ups and downs. "Everything that's happened in my career, onscreen and offscreen, we've always done it together." Their plan was to have both biological and adopted children. When Deb finished shooting *Fire,* she largely put her career on hold to focus on starting their family.

Beauty and the Beast transferred to Sydney for a few months, then wrapped in June 1996, and because of his success as Gaston, Hugh was asked to audition for *Sunset Boulevard* at the Regent Theatre in Melbourne. He was initially hesitant, not wanting to limit his career by developing a reputation as a "song and dance man." But upon learning Trevor Nunn was directing, who had previously been Artistic Director of the Royal Shakespeare Company in London, he readily agreed to audition, even though he had no intention of accepting the role if offered. Meeting Trevor fit with Hugh's dream of someday performing at the Royal National Theatre.

Thank you, vision board, for the guidance. Keeping your dreams in focus leads you to the right opportunities.

When Hugh talked about that audition, you could see in his eyes and hear in his voice the energy that makes him such an exciting actor. He described how Trevor set him up: "There's 1200 people out there who hate you. You've got three minutes to convince every one of them otherwise. Go!" Hugh realized very quickly that he would take any role offered for the chance to work closely with Trevor. That wise choice would lead to his career expanding outside Australia the following year, fulfilling his dream of the National Theatre in London.

Trevor recognized the "it factor" in Hugh, the "aura that separates the lead from the chorus." The renowned director raved about Hugh's "level of detail and finesse." Hugh's co-star, Debra Byrne, said, "He's incredibly talented – and so fresh, so excited, and just as scared as I am." As part of his preparation, he got to come to New York for the first time, to see *Sunset Boulevard* on Broadway. I can only imagine how much fun they had, Deb showing him around the city she'd fallen in love with. They stood in line three mornings in a row to get standing room tickets to see Al Pacino in *Hughie* on Broadway. On the third day they were finally successful, but Deb was so tired after repeatedly getting up early, she fell asleep shortly after the performance started! That experience (the waiting in line part, not the falling asleep part) inspired Deb to write and later direct the short film, *Standing Room Only.*

Then from October 1996 to June 1997, Hugh played the dashing Joe Gillis eight times a week, earning Variety Club and Mo awards. He credits Trevor with giving him the confidence that he could achieve anything he wanted, that he deserved to act anywhere – London's West End, on Broadway, in Hollywood, wherever he wanted.

Mentors who see your potential before you can see it are so valuable. On the title page of this book I credit my mentor, Dana, who believed in me as an author long before I did. If you don't have a mentor or boss who sees the best in you and encourages you, find one. Soon.

Which is not to say it always felt easy. Hugh describes live theatre as, "It is like bungee jumping. And that's why I love it. I love the thrill of it. But sometimes it scares the hell out of you."

*So how does the Joy Revolution relate to getting out of your comfort zone and facing your fear and all that? Let's look again at those emotions. Fear combined with excitement is completely different from fear mixed with dread. The first one signals you to get your autopilot brain focused toward the best possible outcome, which will lead you to prepare like crazy, then go for it! The second signals you to change course and try something different. One of the best descriptions of this balance came from Jerry Hicks, using a basketball analogy. He says to **stand far enough back from the basket that it will give you a thrill when you make it, but not so far that you don't believe it's possible**. Isn't that a great description of the sweet spot?*

Australia would have loved to see Hugh continue right on in musical theater, but he turned down starring in *The Boy from Oz* to pursue film acting. He did go see that show after it opened and realized what a fun role it was. He absolutely made the right career move then, but we're so glad he jumped at the chance to play Peter Allen on Broadway when it was offered five years later!

The first full-length movie Hugh was cast in was *Erskineville Kings*, quite a striking contrast from musicals. The director said when he told people he'd found "this great actor, Hugh Jackman" they'd say "Isn't he a song and dance guy?" Alan would respond, "No, he's a great actor." (Some people think of musicals as entertainment, not acting. So wrong! Musicals done well are a demanding combination of both!) But Hugh wasn't kidding when he said about the movie role, "That required a level of acting that I hadn't been asked to do—that I knew I could do, but I hadn't been asked to do it yet." It's raw and gritty. The film starts slowly but then takes the audience on quite an emotional ride. "I invested my heart into that film. And I probably did exorcise a few demons, maybe some I didn't realize were there," regarding his own mother's leaving. The show was filmed in three weeks, working seven days a week. That would have been an INTENSE three weeks. Some still consider this movie to be among Hugh's best performances.

Hugh reached his largest audience up to that point when he was asked to sing the Australian national anthem on July 26, 1997, at the Bledisloe Cup, a rugby match between Australia and New Zealand. He thought it was funny that he was introduced as a "star of stage and screen" since it was so early in his career, but I think it makes perfect sense, given how people were already reacting to his performances! He said it was one of the most nerve-wracking moments of his life, that he had the only panic attack he's ever had the night before. Waiting in the locker room before he was introduced, he remembers a janitor saying he looked "toey" (nervous). The guy didn't help matters by reminding Hugh there were millions of people watching live on television! Ironically, what grounded him was the enormous chorus of BOOOOs from the New Zealand fans when he was introduced. His competitiveness was ignited, and he sang brilliantly. Based on that performance he was invited to sing at the Melbourne Cup (a horse race) that November.

They spent some time in Brisbane while Deb was filming the movie *The Real Macaw.* Unfortunately, it wasn't an easy time in their lives as getting pregnant wasn't going as smoothly as they had hoped. They tried in-vitro fertilization, which any couple who's been there will tell you is an exhausting process. After going through the heartache of miscarriage twice, they adjusted their original plan and started looking into adoption.

While doing more movie and TV auditions, Hugh was hired as a host of the TV show *In Fashion*. He served as the lay-person whose job it was to ask his fashion expert co-host leading questions. It was on this show that he met Rove McManus, who would go on to host a talk show on which Hugh would appear many times. *In Fashion* wasn't exactly Hugh's proudest work, but it provides priceless comedic material for interviews! It came up several times on *Rove Live*.

Also on TV, it was Hugh's turn to be in an episode of *Halifax F.P.* as the dashing police detective Eric Ringer. Detective Eric had better luck coming on to forensic psychologist Dr. Jane Halifax than the lesbian cop Deb had played a few seasons prior. Rebecca Gibney, who plays Jane, had been good friends with Deb for years. Hugh's episode, titled Afraid of the Dark, included his first on-screen love-making scene, and apparently newlywed Hugh was hesitant during filming. Rebecca told him to "close your eyes and think of Deb." (I'll pause for your collective "Awwwww...") Judging by the end result, that advice worked! The episode aired the following fall and was later released on DVD as *Profile of a Serial Killer*.

Hugh's first adventure as host of an awards show was the Australian Film Institute Awards on November 14, 1997. (Many viewers were surprised by Hugh's charming, cheeky, and impressive opening number when he hosted the Oscars in 2009. Australians weren't. They had seen the singing, dancing, and comedy more than ten years before with The Opening Song.) The five-year-old who stood on a chair and yelled for attention had grown into a performer who could thrive in front of an audience of millions. He charmed a huge crowd again that Christmas Eve hosting Carols by Candlelight in Melbourne.

It's interesting that in an interview just before that performance, he mentioned his desire to record an original music album. He's a Grammy winner now thanks to the *Showman* soundtrack, but might we finally get that solo album in conjunction with his 2019 World Tour?

You never know how or when dreams will come true!

Hugh and Deb were visiting Hugh's mum and sisters in the UK, and he contacted Trevor Nunn to see if he could audition while he was there. Trevor asked him to come in the next day (!) with a Shakespeare monologue and a song to be considered for *Oklahoma!* They went to a bookstore to get a copy of *Henry IV Part 1*, then spent four hours in a park with Deb helping him prepare. His monologue was "My liege, I did deny no prisoners..." For the song he chose "Oh What a Beautiful Morning." Part way through the audition he forgot the words, but the panel all started singing along! He figured he had either really bombed or that the part was his. (It was the latter, of course.)

That offer brought about a dilemma, because Deb had just been offered a spot in the directing program at the Victorian College of the Arts in Melbourne. The prestigious program was very difficult to get into, and directing a full-length movie was (and still is!) one of Deb's big dreams. Hugh said he would turn down London for Deb to pursue that program, but she said, "No, we need to go." The depth and strength of their partnership is evident here in two ways. First, doing both and being separated wasn't even considered as an option. Second, they had made a pact when they got married to always consider the good of the family at each turning point. Even though kids hadn't joined the family yet, they were already a factor in the decision. They were pursuing adoption and Deb knew she wanted the kids to be her primary focus when they arrived. So following the avenues that opened in Hugh's career made sense. I would have done the same thing, no question. But I still want to see Deb direct a feature film! I hope that's her first empty nest project.

Once again we see them using dreams as a guide. There were three dreams in play here—Hugh at the National Theatre, Deb studying directing, and them becoming parents. Going to London was the clear choice because the dream of motherhood was the stronger pull for Deb at the time. I can relate. I infamously said to my now-husband on our second date, "You need to know I'm nowhere near ready for a serious relationship, but having said that, are you interested in having more kids?" During my first marriage I had resigned myself to likely not ever being a mom. Then I found a lump in my breast and my instinctive response was, "You can't cut into me there, I haven't fed my babies yet." I did end up having the benign lump removed, but it was a blinding flash of clarity, so when I had a second chance to choose a partner, that was one of my top criteria. I figured I may as well be straightforward up front that it was a deal breaker!

Deb and Hugh had started inquiring about adopting a baby in Australia but were shocked at how inhospitable the system was. There were many hoops to jump through, and people seemed more interested in putting up roadblocks than in facilitating the process of matching them up with a baby in need of a home. Since Deb had a green card from her work in the US, they started looking into the process there, and found a much warmer reception.

March of 1998 brought the filming of Hugh's second movie, *Paperback Hero,* in Queensland. His first foray into romantic comedy did not disappoint. Andrew Urban, a reporter on set, described him thus: "Hugh, tall and every inch of him leading man material, has an intelligence and warmth that mix with a masculinity that is highlighted in these conditions, his singlet stained with the sweat of his work." Director Antony Bowman agreed. "I can't tell you how good these actors are. They've made the characters their own – all of them. Now I'm just guiding them through."

Then off they went to London! The Royal National Theatre – Hugh's vision board was coming true much more quickly than he could have imagined. Rehearsals started in April with Maureen Lipman co-starring as Aunt Eller.

Since they were fairly close by, Hugh and Deb popped over to the Cannes Film Festival in May to see if they could find a distributor for *Paperback Hero.* They stayed in a youth hostel and strategized about getting into parties without invitations. Thanks to Deb, who always believes anything is possible, they were pretty successful! It would be quite a different story when they attended again eight years later, as parents of two small children, with both of them promoting major movies they had starred in, staying in a luxury suite in a swanky hotel!

Back in London, at the first preview performance on July 6, Hugh's adrenaline was running a little high. During the dream ballet he is meant to lift Laurey up to his shoulder, but he used a little too much force and threw her across the room behind him! "Oh, sh*#! Sorry!" he exclaimed loudly into his stage mic. The show ran July 15—October 3 at the National Theatre, then transferred to the Lyceum Theatre in January. In between, the cast filmed the stage-to-screen version that we are SO grateful for because we still get to enjoy it today!

The role of Curly brought Hugh into international awareness as an actor. One reviewer described, "His legs are as high as an elephant's eye. When he walks onto the stage singing, a soft female sigh runs nightly round the packed auditorium. The man is 29 and irresistible." Hugh claims it was a "lean year" at home because Deb wasn't a fan of his permed hair. Yeah, right. We're not buying it. Especially when Deb raved about her husband in the role. "He represented everything this character portrayed. [Curly] was fresh... full of hope and idealism, and I think Hugh has a lot of those qualities."

Queen Elizabeth and Prince Philip loved the performance. Evidently it brought back memories of seeing the original production when they were dating. Princess Margaret came to see the show nine times. She found Hugh as irresistible as the rest of us do! He received a well-deserved nomination for an Olivier Award, the UK equivalent of a Tony Award. Success with critics and fans on stage doesn't translate into wealth though. While Deb and Hugh were blissfully happy in London, Deb says "We were poor. We used to save up to buy raspberries." Hugh agrees that their level of happiness hasn't been defined by money. In 2013 he said, "I don't think, either, that money has made me any more happy than I was when I was earning £375 a week in *Oklahoma!* at the National. Debs and I had a great time then, and we have a great time now."

Read that again. When you're happy regardless of your level of wealth, money flows more easily. When you're stressed about money, your autopilot brain is pointed toward not-enough-money and you might not notice opportunities that would change that.

That December they squeezed in a trip home to Australia, and Hugh treated us to a little Disney magic hosting Carols in the Domain at the Domain gardens in Sydney. David Hobson and Peter Cousen collaborated with Hugh that night for a charming rendition of "We Three Kings." On New Year's Eve, Hugh was asked to be the host of the Sydney celebration, which included ad libbed commentary during the fireworks show. The event staff assured him they had plenty of background information he could use to fill up the time. But just as the fireworks display started, Hugh saw a drunk crew member light his notes on fire. He calls that the worst 45 minutes of his life, and is glad his days of having to say yes to any paying gig are over. But once again, it's great fodder for laughs on talk shows now!

In January 1999, just as *Oklahoma!* was getting going in its Lyceum run, there was a worldwide casting call for the part of Wolverine in *X-Men.* The director had wanted Russell Crowe for the part, but when Russell decided he wasn't interested, the studio opted to look for an unknown actor. Russell said they should take special notice of his buddy Jacko. What followed was the famous "one time" in their marriage that Deb was wrong. Looking at the character description, Deb thought it was "ridiculous" for Hugh to go from being on stage in London's West End to playing a mutant with metal claws. But Hugh's overriding "Have a go!" philosophy of life won out. Plus, he figured if Ian McKellen and Patrick Stewart were involved, it couldn't be too ridiculous...

So he did a screen test between a Wednesday matinee and evening performance, with his Curly perm and southern cowboy accent (because that was the only American accent he knew at that point.) The tight schedule ended up working to Hugh's advantage. They were running late, as is common, but Hugh values punctuality, so he was irritated. Knowing the window of time was closing before he had to be on stage that evening, he knocked on the door and told them he had to go next or he couldn't go at all. And during the reading, he was a little impatient and demanding, wanting to get through both scenes in the time he had. Excellent temperament for Wolverine! It resulted in a call back the next day.

Can I stop and point out that being nice doesn't mean not standing up for yourself? I'm guessing the confidence Trevor Nunn had inspired in Hugh was part of what allowed him to be assertive in fitting in his audition before he had to go back to work!

In March of 1999, *Paperback Hero* was released. It's known as "Jackman's first film" because it was released before *Erskineville Kings*, even though it was the second one he shot. In any case, his big screen debut was VERY well received!

On a break from the London production, Hugh came to Los Angeles to see about finding an agent in Hollywood. He met with Creative Artists Agency (CAA) last, figuring the biggest agency was a long shot for him. Turns out, they were courting Hugh based on the recommendation of Nicole Kidman and Tom Cruise, and on reaction to his performances in London and in his first movie! Patrick Whitesell was the agent he chose to work with. Hugh made sure Patrick understood he didn't want to limit himself to movies, he still wanted to do stage work, too. Patrick has been on board from the beginning with Hugh's desire for variety, and to choose projects that sound fun, even if they're not always logical.

Your key advisors need to be on board with the Joy Revolution.

Since it was Hugh's first trip to Los Angeles, but Deb had lived there previously, she loved showing him the sites. The first landmark she took him to was Grauman's Chinese Theatre, and he remembers putting his hands in Peter Sellers' handprints. Was he dreaming about someday having his own hand and footprints there? Could he have imagined that it would happen just ten years later?

Just like Hugh's photo of himself in front of the Royal National Theatre in London, he was creating a new vision board with new dreams.

With his new agent's guidance, Hugh ended up being one of the finalists for the role of Wolverine, and the studio wanted to fly him to Los Angeles for another audition. Hugh wasn't willing to miss performances of *Oklahoma!* for that (he didn't even miss performances when he had a migraine) so the studio agreed to fly him over on the Concorde so the timing could work. It sounds like Hugh was even more excited about the flight experience than the short list audition! Unfortunately things kept coming up that made the studio postpone that audition five weeks in a row, then the director decided to cast Dougray Scott for the part. I'm pretty sure Hugh was more bummed about not getting the Concorde ride than about not getting the role! Ah well, back to the ho hum life of starring in a hit West End musical...

As *Oklahoma!* neared the end of its run, the exhausted cast started to get a little punchy. In her book *Lip Reading,* Maureen Lipman described how the other cast members backstage tried to throw Hugh off his game whenever he faced the wings: lewd poses, random costume pieces worn in ridiculous ways, a line of cowboys dropping their chaps in a synchronized mooning, even props discarded from other shows made their way into the debauchery. But Hugh "had a way of incorporating open-mouthed laughter into Curly's sheer pleasure in the actual moment as envisaged by Rodgers & Hammerstein." And here's my favorite story from Maureen:

> On the last matinee I dressed Hugh's real-life wife, Deb, in my first-act costume and as he sang 'Don't throw bouquets at me...' she stood in the wings brandishing a rolling pin. Hugh was captivated. Just clapped his hands and laughed out loud. As we all piled on stage to congratulate him and Laurey, there was one tall, statuesque blonde in a lace 'fascinator' who got more than the average hug and kiss.

There are a few more sweet tidbits in Maureen's book. Speaking of a night they were raising money for charity, she said, "I'd sent Hugh out into the audience to auction his body (I was prepared to go up to seven million myself)." We hear you, sister. And referring to her tears in the final curtain call of the final show, "I clung onto Hugh, the best on-stage partner I'd known." That's quite a compliment from a woman who had already spent 32 years on the stage.

So what does a guy do when he's 29 and has achieved his biggest dream? He started to realize the possibilities for the future were literally beyond his wildest dreams. Trevor gave Hugh some career advice during that time that he never forgot. "When the demands of the part and your potential meet, then you're onto something." *It sounds like the same sentiment as Jerry Hicks' advice on how far away from the basket to stand.*

Lest we start thinking Hugh's career has been all roses, the refusal of American Equity to allow the London production to transfer to Broadway was a disappointment to the whole cast. Hugh auditioned for *Moulin Rouge* around this time but didn't get the role. (He was in good company as Leonardo DiCaprio, Heath Ledger, and Jake Gyllenhaal all lost out to Ewan McGregor.) Combined with someone else being chosen for the part of Wolverine, Hugh would have been justified in holding a bit of a pity party. But it appears he took it all in stride as just part of the business, and he and Deb went back to Australia to see what would come up next!

Deb filmed an episode of *Sea Change,* then in September of 1999, *Erskineville Kings* was (finally) released. Hugh was nominated for an Australian Film Institute Best Actor award and won the Film Critics Circle of Australia Best Actor award for that performance, beating out fellow nominee Heath Ledger. The director, Alan White, asked Hugh if he would appear in another film, which would start shooting in October, and Hugh agreed.

In an interview at that time, Hugh said he and Deb had decided they would split their time between Los Angeles and Australia since Hollywood is the worldwide center of the film industry. I'm guessing this decision also had to do with them being approved as adoptive parents in the US!

In late September Hugh again sang the Australian national anthem at a major sporting event, this time the National Rugby League Grand Final. He won the Australian Star of the Year at the Australian Movie Convention, joining illustrious previous winners such as Russell Crowe, Hugo Weaving, and Geoffrey Rush. Trevor Nunn said, "In my view there is an enormous future for Hugh, and I'm just going to be part of the group doing the scramble trying to get to him." Hugh and Deb were feeling pretty optimistic.

But could they even imagine that less than a year later Hugh would be a world-wide superstar?

CHAPTER 5

LEVELING UP

What began as a rushed audition with a baseball cap covering his curly hair became the biggest break of Hugh's career. In the fall of 1999, before he started filming his friend's movie in Australia, Hugh and Deb came to Los Angeles to meet with an adoption attorney. Hugh called his agent to see if there was anything he could read for while he was in town. Patrick had just heard Dougray Scott might have to pull out of *X-Men,* so he sent Hugh to meet with the studio. After four days of meetings, they flew him to Toronto to read for the director, Bryan Singer.

The other actors in *X-Men* were charmed by Hugh within a few minutes. Patrick Stewart recalls that they were "running out of stuff to shoot without someone to play Logan," then this "really cute Australian guy" came in to read for the part. But after his reading, Hugh told them "you'll never see me again." Evidently Bryan is a closed book during auditions, so even if he's really pleased, the actors rarely know. Plus Bryan still thought Dougray was Plan A and Hugh only represented an overzealous studio wanting a Plan B. But a few days later they flew him back to Toronto again for a screen test on set, and his agent started negotiating in case he was chosen. While he was performing with Anna Paquin, a custodian tapped Singer on the shoulder and asked if "that guy" was going to play Wolverine. Figuring that was a good test balloon, Bryan said yes and the crewman said, "Cool!" It must have been the icing on the cake, because Hugh was offered the role at the end of that day! Bryan says it's the only time he's ever hired an actor on the spot. (Well, nine months after Hugh's first audition...)

But wait. Hugh had promised to shoot a movie with his friend in Australia, starting in less than two weeks. *X-Men* needed him to start immediately.

Hugh shared this story for the first time in 2018, to illustrate how much he respects Patrick and appreciates him as a friend and advisor. In Hugh's first project with a big-time Hollywood agent, he assumed he would get pressure to take the high-dollar gig. Patrick assured Hugh they would honor his commitment to his friend, because "Where you want to get to in life is never as important as the way you want to live your life." The greatest opportunity in the world isn't worth it if you let down the friend who cast you in your first movie role.

Wow. (Would this be the time for me to proudly mention that Patrick is a fellow Iowan?)

Thankfully, when Patrick explained Hugh's opportunity to Alan, he happily cast someone else in the role he had intended for Hugh, and Wolverine was on! Not only did that LA trip result in a successful meeting about adoption, their worries about the expense of adoption were in the past thanks to *X-Men*. Being a newbie, Hugh was astounded when Patrick said they had negotiated the studio DOWN from three pictures to two! "They were offering me three???" he said. He soon figured out how deal-making works, but he has wisely let Patrick handle the details his whole career. Hugh began rehearsals and action choreography (and workouts, and growing mutton chops!) on October 11, 1999. Hugh and Deb had only packed for a week in Los Angeles, so they had to buy warmer clothes for the snow in Toronto!

But there was one other obligation Hugh had to attend to before he could dedicate himself fully to filming. Fox Studios Australia, recognizing his stage charisma, had booked him to host their grand opening in November. He sang with Shirley Jones, who played Laurey in the film version of *Oklahoma!* in 1955. Hugh couldn't hide his elation at getting to perform with such an icon! (Shirley seemed pretty elated herself.) Many Australian actors were there, and since Mission Impossible II was being shot there, Dougray Scott was at the event as well. Hugh was worried it would be awkward so approached him and started to say "Hey, listen, I'm sorry..." but Dougray cut him off with "No, no. Forget that. It's show biz, this stuff happens. But you happen to have one of the best parts I've ever read. Go crush it."

There was a lot to adjust to during Hugh's first experience in a Hollywood production. "I remember the first night I filmed: It was an outdoor sequence at the train station, and I remember pulling up and it was like a Rolling Stones concert. It was 400 cast and crew. My trailer was the size of my pub back at home, and I was like, 'Whoa.'"

When Hugh first walked on set in costume, a crew member blurted out, "Elvis is in the building." Bryan Singer overheard that comment and shut down filming for five hours while they went back to the drawing board (or the makeup trailer as it were) for Wolverine's hair.

Along with differences in the size of the production and the amenities on set, relationships are different on a Hollywood set. The crew are trained to keep their distance from the stars, but that wasn't Hugh's style. Looking for a graceful way to get to know people, he invented an "Australian tradition" where an actor buys lottery tickets for the crew every Friday. Of course this "tradition" became extremely popular, but an unintended consequence has been that Hugh is ALWAYS on every Friday's call sheet in every movie he's been in! Incidentally, he readily acknowledges that his experience has proven the adage that the lottery is a tax on people who are bad at math. It has been fruitful for building friendships. For building capital? Not so much.

And how about the actual work of acting in a big Hollywood movie? It didn't go smoothly at first. The studio and the director weren't seeing the spark they'd seen in Hugh's audition. Hugh was frustrated because he was trying so hard to do everything the director wanted. *Note: trying really hard tends to be the opposite of spark.* The turning point came through Deb. She encouraged him to stop listening to all the voices around him and trying to please everyone else, and to start really focusing on being the character and trusting his instincts. Hugh recognized her wisdom and thought, "So I'm just going to do what I want. If I go down, I'll go down swinging, not feeling meek."

The biggest challenge for Hugh was figuring out how to bury his usual joyfulness. As his brother said when he got cast, "You? Wolverine? You were never even in trouble at school! No one's going to believe you're Wolverine!" He had to find a way to portray perpetual grumpiness. One morning he happened to get blasted with cold water in the shower, but he stifled any reaction so as not to wake Deb. He realized the way he felt in that moment was perfect for his character. So for the rest of the filming he blasted himself with cold water on occasion to feed that underlying irritation. He also drew inspiration from watching Mel Gibson in *Road Warrior.* Mad Max's man-of-few-words-but-you-sure-know-his-mood style was the missing piece that helped Hugh capture the aura of a character who knows he has lived hundreds of years of pain and violence but can't remember any of it.

It worked. The director was much happier!

Another Joy Revolution milestone: trusting your gut enough to change up what doesn't feel right to you instead of trying to second-guess what others are wanting.

He was his usual jovial self between takes, though, with a lot of singing and dancing. When he started doing some moves from Michael Jackson's *Thriller* and got only blank stares, he realized just how young Anna Paquin was. (And how young he wasn't anymore!)

Hugh had put on muscle for roles before, but playing Wolverine took things to a whole new level. Since they had already started filming the movie when he got cast, there wasn't time for him to bulk up before he jumped in. So the cage fight scene was filmed at the end of the schedule, five months later, after he had time to develop that impressive torso. And even then, Hugh exceeded their expectations. It wasn't initially planned as a shirtless scene, but Hugh came in and said he'd really been hitting the gym hard, and he thought it would be more effective without a shirt – could they try it for a few takes? I can't imagine it now without seeing Wolverine's raw power, can you?

As an action movie, the stunts were definitely beyond what Hugh had experienced before. A reporter asked if he did a lot of them himself?

> *I did do a lot, and I had a fantastic double who did a lot. Usually the routine was this: They would say, 'Now this is kind of a dangerous stunt,' and I would say, "OK, Steve (the double), you do it, and let me have a look at it in rehearsal, and I'll see if I can do it.' ... I'd look and I'd go, 'Oh yeah, I can do that. Save Steve for the really hard stuff.' So I'd get in and do it. And I realized how hard and difficult and how much it was hurting, and that these guys, these stunt doubles, they just never show pain.*

We have to wonder about the studio's wisdom in letting him try some of the stunts, since Hugh admits he's a bit of a klutz. Which means the claws were a bit too realistic as well. Hugh cut himself with them on his face and arms, then famously stabbed the Mystique stunt double during a fight scene. Hugh was horrified, but she raised her arm in the air with a triumphant whoop. "I've been stabbed by Wolverine!"

62

We all find joy in different ways... ☺

With co-stars like Ian McKellan, Patrick Stewart, and Halle Berry, Hugh was pretty surprised to have top billing. He told his agent the billing didn't seem right, because "Ian McKellan is a hero of mine. I've watched him on stage for years, I've seen him on tapes. He's the best Macbeth ever."

Patrick said, "Don't argue." Right!

The thrill of wrapping his first Hollywood film was eclipsed by another dream that came true for Hugh and Deb – becoming parents. They were matched with a baby-to-be and even got to be present in the delivery room when Oscar was born. Hugh recalled that Deb was trying to capture the moment in pictures, as she loves to do, but she was so emotional they all turned out blurry. Deb's mother had flown over from Australia for the occasion and remembered Deb running down the hallway into the waiting room with tears streaming down her cheeks exclaiming "I've just had a boy!" (Others in the waiting room were confused that she could be up and running around so quickly, until Fay explained they were adopting.) Deb has said that she's a big believer in destiny – that we choose our parents, even if we don't find them the traditional way. I wholeheartedly agree.

During the filming Hugh had done several recordings of dialogue for use in video games and toys. How endearing for their son to have a figurine (that he loved!!) with his father's voice saying "I'm gonna slice you in half!"

On the *X-Men* press junket, a reporter asked Hugh to sing, and he happily obliged, convincing Anna Paquin to join him in a rendition of "Oh What a Beautiful Morning." The studio wasn't too delighted with the joyful, musical version of their anti-hero... But Hugh is who he is! The premiere was a pretty wild extravaganza on Ellis Island. And since the movie had been rushed to market, everyone was seeing the final version with special effects for the first time.

Comic book movies were not expected to be blockbusters at that point. In fact, people close to Hugh warned him to be sure to have his next movie role locked in before *X-Men* came out, so he wasn't negotiating with a bomb hanging over his head. (He followed that advice and did lots of auditions. In fact, he was already filming *Someone Like You* when *X-Men* opened.) But Deb knew better. "My wife is unbelievably prescient with these things—she gets a sense of what's happening way before I do. On that opening weekend, we stood on a stoop on a Saturday night, and she said, 'Everything's different from here'. I'm like, 'C'mon it's just one film,

Deb'. She wasn't having it. 'No, I can feel it. It's changed. It's all going to change from here.'"

The movie opened July 14, 2000. Within a few days, paparazzi were capturing Hugh's daily moves and he began to field fan interactions on the street on a regular basis. And they weren't necessarily all happy, admiring fans. Comic book aficionados had lots to say about what Hugh should have done differently playing their beloved Wolverine, starting with being a foot shorter. Hugh remembers thinking, "How the hell do you know where I am all the time? I don't even know where I'm going. What's going on here?" On July 25, Hugh appeared on an American talk show for the first time, with Jay Leno.

Of course there were many adoring fans as well, such as the young restaurant manager in Tribeca who was so excited and nervous to have Hugh and Deb in his establishment he was sweating, then whipped off his shirt to show a huge X-Men tattoo on his back.

It wasn't just fans who took notice. Prior to the release of *X-Men,* Hugh auditioned against thirty or forty other actors for every role. After that point, most offers came in with no audition required. One of the first calls that came was from John Travolta, wanting to cast Hugh in his upcoming movie, *Swordfish,* which would start filming as soon as *Someone Like You* wrapped. JT had gone to see *X-Men* in the theater and was captivated by Hugh on screen, comparing him to a young Clint Eastwood or Sean Connery.

Patrick told Hugh he could probably jump right into "name above title" roles, but he would rather have Hugh get more experience in film through working alongside seasoned movie actors. In *Someone Like You*, originally titled *Animal Husbandry,* Hugh was getting to learn from Ashley Judd. *Swordfish* was a fantastic opportunity to get to know and learn from John Travolta. Soon after that, with *Kate & Leopold*, he would get to expand his experience in comedy alongside Meg Ryan.

Around this time, Hugh was offered the lead in *Chicago*. Even though he had been wanting to do a movie musical, he turned it down. They had a brand new baby so things were busy, but mostly he couldn't get past the idea that he was too young for the role. The line "I've seen it all, kid" just didn't make sense when Hugh was the same age as the other characters in the story. But as he watched that film in the theater, then saw Richard Gere receive a Best Actor Golden Globe and the film win the Oscar for Best Picture, he was wishing he'd thought of putting on makeup to make himself look older!

Of course Deb was loving Hugh's sky rocketing success, but she was also pleased that his new roles were clean shaven. She wasn't a fan of the Wolverine mutton chops.

Hugh and Ashley and Greg Kinnear and Marisa Tomei had an absolute blast filming *Someone Like You.* They played charades between takes, and the whole process was very creative. "A lot of things were being changed and made up" as they went, Hugh said, including Ashley's late-night cheer.

The whirlwind adventure continued as he jumped straight into filming *Swordfish.* He had been star struck working with Ian McKellen, and now he was working with another of his heroes. Hugh raves about John Travolta's talent, then sums it up with, "He's just so much fun! The guy has far too much fun. He's like a little kid. We ended up singing together off camera, doing songs from *Grease*, singing Sinatra, we just had a ball!" (Makes perfect sense on this intense action flick...) John was a valuable mentor to Hugh, not only in acting, but in how to gracefully handle fame— finding a balance between making fans happy and being able to do your job and live your life. John says fame just makes you more of who you are. If you're a kind person, you'll be ten times kinder. If you're an asshole, you'll be ten times worse. Obviously Hugh is the former, and John taught him how to keep living a normal life in the midst of celebrity.

Swordfish was filmed partly on location in Oregon and partly in a studio in California. Deb and Oscar went along wherever Hugh was working. One of the funny stories Hugh told about that project was filming the scene where he was left alone with a fancy computer system, and the script simply said to "hack brilliantly." There was no dialogue, and Hugh had no idea how to act hacking. They ended up asking a computer guru to sit underneath the desk while they were filming to suggest different words and actions. It was helpful, although I'm guessing the dancing part was all Hugh.

Hugh's mastery of different American accents was increasing with every project. But there were a few lines that tripped him up, like the word murderer. He later told Ellen Degeneres, "There's like eleven Rs in that word!" The other line that drove him crazy was "Who are we at war with?" Definitely a tongue twister for someone not used to putting an R sound before another consonant.

One day John told Hugh to stop in his trailer after lunch. Hugh was completely blown away to come face to face with Olivia Newton-John. He'd had a major crush on her as a teen, so being in the same room with Danny *and* Sandy, Hugh's mind exploded a little. He blurted out to Olivia that he'd had a poster of her on his bedroom wall, and he would kiss it every morning. Hugh says Olivia looked embarrassed, but I'm willing to bet she thought it was a sweet story. We'll call that Episode 1 of What Not To Do When You Meet Your Heroes. (I'm guessing Hugh has also been on the receiving end of a lot of those moments in the past 20 years.)

Although his career developments were pretty exciting, Hugh lit up like a Christmas tree when he talked about life as a husband and father. "Oscar has changed my life completely and beautifully and brilliantly. And my kid is just, of course, the most amazing kid of all time." Even though journalists were trying to ask him about his movies, stories about Deb and Oscar kept working themselves in. Deb happened to be visiting him on set the day they filmed the first hacking scene, where there is a gun to his head and a woman's head in his lap. The woman was horrified to be shooting that scene in front of her co-star's wife. But Hugh LOVES telling the story. "Well, Deb just walked up to the actress and said, 'Hi, I believe that you're the one who is making out with my husband today.' This poor girl turned around and said, 'Yes, I'm so sorry.' And my wife went, 'What are you sorry for? You're getting paid for it. Nobody pays me to hop into bed with him.'"

Filming wrapped in mid-December in time for a holiday break. After a very eventful year, they went home to Australia to introduce Oscar to their extended family.

Filming of *Kate & Leopold* began in February of 2001 in New York. Deb and Oscar stayed close by of course – there are some adorable photos of Hugh in his Leopold costume playing with baby Oscar. *Someone Like You* was released at the end of March, so Hugh took a break from filming to do publicity. Then back at work, Hugh and Meg did the horse riding through Central Park themselves and loved every minute! They both appreciated each other's down-to-earth-ness, but Hugh also was learning a lot. "[In Meg] you see the consummate professional – a comedienne who knows technically as much as instinctively and creatively what to do with a scene. She's very generous, she's very helpful." Hugh would work with Liev Schreiber again on the first Wolverine spin-off, and with James Mangold as director again on the second and third Wolverine films.

Kate & Leopold wrapped in May, then in June, *Swordfish* was released and Hugh made his second appearance on *The Tonight Show*. A few days later at the Saturn Awards, Hugh won Best Actor for *X-Men*. Things were cooking!

After jumping in the deep end of Hollywood, filming four hit movies in less than two years, Hugh and Deb took some downtime to enjoy being a family of three. Then before he knew it, it was time to do press for *Kate & Leopold*'s release! Hugh hosted *Saturday Night Live* on December 8. He hadn't really been familiar with the show, but his "have a go" spirit served him well! He treated the audience to his gorgeous baritone rendition of "Have Yourself a Merry Little Christmas" in the opening. Skits included the ribald story of the Christmas Kangaroo, Hugh as a beautiful young model visiting Donatella Versace in her bathtub, and (my favorite) Superman Hugh in an awkward phone conversation with his mom, dad, and grandma. A few days later he appeared on Jay Leno's show for the third time in 18 months!

A nice Christmas present that year was the announcement on December 20 that Hugh was nominated for a Best Actor Golden Globe for his portrayal of Leopold! The movie was officially released on Christmas Day. Awards night was January 20, and Hugh and Deb were glowing on the red carpet taking in the mania that greeted them as everyone's favorite newcomers to the scene.

I'm a fan of romantic comedies, and I saw both *Someone Like You* and *Kate & Leopold* around the same time, but I never realized the same actor was in both. Hugh completely embodies the characters he's playing! Seeing Leopold first, I assumed Hugh was a buttoned-up British actor so I didn't see any resemblance to Eddie the cigarette-smoking playboy New Yorker. And if I had been an *X-Men* fan at the time, I certainly wouldn't have connected either Leopold or Eddie with Wolverine, nor would I have ever imagined the actor playing all three was Australian!

In March of 2002, Hugh co-presented with Naomi Watts at the Oscars, in the category of Best Animated Short Film. John Travolta had given him the advice to treat every public speaking opportunity with respect, whether you had 20 seconds at the microphone or a starring role, and he did. No show stealing, but a solid "And the Oscar goes to..." followed by a handshake and handing over the statuette. His comment that night was, "There'll be a lot of drunken parties back home and people betting and that's usually what I'm at, so getting up there in a suit and talking for a little bit is kind of bizarre."

Around that time Hugh was asked if he was interested in being the next James Bond. After some discussion back and forth, including a question on his part about how much artistic input he would have in the storyline (the answer was none), he took his name out of the running. Being part of two major franchises would have limited his other options, and he wasn't as excited about the Bond scripts as he was about the direction *X-Men* was going. These days some fans wonder, now that he's done playing Wolverine, can we revisit that 007 question?

Deb had found the funding to make her short film, *Standing Room Only*, so they shot it that spring while they were in London. She wanted Michael Gambon to be in it, but friends told her that was out of her league. *Deb always believes anything is possible.* So she asked, and he said yes! Deb said it was her favorite project of her career up to that point. "I loved having a vision and then when you get a whole team of people to realize your vision and it comes to life, it is beyond exhilarating." She certainly does appear to be a natural born director, as Hugh calls her. I love her perspective on being a devoted mom but also putting on her oxygen mask. "It is all about balance. Family always comes first but part of me is the actor so if I don't let that live I am letting my kids down as well."

In June Hugh sang in the United States for the first time. He was invited to perform the lead role in a concert version of *Carousel* in Carnegie Hall as part of the celebration of Richard Rodgers' 100th birthday. (When his appearance had been announced in February, the news release cautioned that it was conditional on the *X-Men 2* shooting schedule.)

When Hugh's dad learned about the *Carousel* performance, he couldn't hide his excitement and made arrangements to fly from Sydney to New York (a 24-hour trek each way). He would be in New York less than a full day, but that way he only had to miss three days of work. As one would expect from an accountant, Chris wanted to know every detail including the exact timeline, dress code, etc. Hugh told him to wear black tie. But after Chris was already on the plane, Hugh found out the dress code was business casual. He panicked, thinking his dad was likely traveling with a tuxedo and shorts and nothing in between. As soon as Chris landed, Hugh called and gave him the update. Chris said he had it covered, then asked if he could meet Hugh at his hotel room and walk him to the stage door. The knock on the door came at the exact appointed time, and Hugh opened it to find his dad wearing a tux. Hugh protested, but Chris said "My son is singing at Carnegie Hall, it is black tie for me." (Go ahead, wipe your eyes.) Hugh sang with Wolverine mutton chops since filming of *X2* started just over a week later.

Leading up to his second Wolverine adventure, there was just one change Hugh wanted. Filming in Toronto in the winter hadn't matched his vision of the Hollywood life. "I think that the movie should be set in a warmer climate. There are some very bad people on the barrier reef, I believe. I, for one, have heard a lot about scuba-diving mutants." Alas, no one else caught that vision. So off the family went to Vancouver. The *X2* plot was kept tightly under wraps, with not even the actors knowing how it ended until they were part way through filming. And shooting the scene where Mystique comes to Wolverine's tent? "It was a tough day at work— three almost naked women on top of me one after the other." Filming wrapped in November and the Jackman family again enjoyed some holiday down time.

Hugh's Hollywood career was on quite a trajectory when he got a call asking if he would play the lead in *The Boy from Oz* on Broadway. Many people told him it was a crazy career move to take 18 months off from movies to be on stage, especially playing a gay entertainer. But Hugh really wanted to do it. He says it was a "turning point, not just career wise, but how I felt. It was a turning point in following and trusting my instincts, because I'd been offered that originally and turned it down." I think he followed his instincts back when he turned it down, too, even if he wasn't doing so consciously. He acknowledges that he likely wouldn't have been cast as Wolverine if he had become known for Peter Allen first.

The naysayers were drowned out by support from two key people: his wife and his agent. Patrick said when actors are lucky enough to feel that "Hell, yes!" feeling about a role (my words, not his), they absolutely need to follow it.

Again, it really helps if the people closest to you are good Joy Revolution partners.

After *X2* wrapped, but before Broadway rehearsals started, Patrick found what he felt was the right opportunity for Hugh's first above-title movie role, *Van Helsing*. "It was different enough from what I'd done before and yet I could tell it was sort of in my strengths," Hugh said. He had been offered another opportunity to work with John Travolta in *The Punisher* at the same time, but turned that one down. The monster-slayer character required hair extensions, which was fine with Hugh because he reports that Deb liked the look. (Deb jokes that being married to Hugh is kind of like having an affair every three months as he changes characters!) So Hugh did publicity for *X-Men 2* looking very un-Wolverine-like, with long beautiful locks.

X-Men 2 premiered in London on April 24, and opened on May 2. It was a record breaker in several ways, opening in at least 80 countries in one day, including almost 3,800 theaters in the US. At that time, Hugh hadn't officially signed on to the third movie in the trilogy (remember that shrewd bargaining on Patrick's part), but producer Lauren Shuler Donner was quoted as saying "We will never do an *X-Men* without Wolverine so production on a third film will depend upon Jackman's availability." That's quite a vote of confidence.

Van Helsing was filmed primarily in Prague and of course Deb and Oscar went along. Oscar was just turning three, and he got to go on set and experiment with flying on the huge soundstage where all of the wire work was done. Normal life for a toddler when Dad's a movie star! People think of Wolverine as Hugh's most physical role, but he recalls that *Van Helsing* was probably 50% tougher than *X-Men* physically. Hugh's stunt double was his sister Sonia's fiance, Richard Bradshaw. Richard broke his leg during filming, but it seems to have healed in time for their late summer wedding! Hugh loves to do as much of the stunt work as he can, but occasionally his clumsy side pops up. I'll let him tell this story:

> *The Czech extras happened to be taken from a homeless shelter. They played the peasants, and they were brilliant by the way. It's great for them because they get 40 or 50 days work a year now that the film industry is booming there. So there's this one scene where the brides are attacking and there's this big melee going on in the village. And I'm running forward to grab onto the legs of Kate Beckinsale who's being dragged off by a wire, so it's very important that I'm staying focused. And this guy runs in front of me and I put my hand out and I just felt him crumple. As I continued on with the take—that sounds terrible, doesn't it—I was thinking, 'I think that guy's in a bad way.' So I went to try and find him and the poor guy was running away from me! He was terrified that the big Hollywood star was going to come and fire him! Of course I just wanted to go and apologize. It ended up he had broken his arm!*
>
> *In the course of that day I knocked over old women, broke a guy's hand, kids, I knocked them all over. I said, 'You know what, if you cut this the right way you could make me the most unlikable hero in movie history.'*

He had a blast with leading lady Kate Beckinsale who of course raved about Hugh. "He's strong and he's fit and he has good humor, and he doesn't give off a sense of arrogance or vanity and yet he's extremely cute as well. So he's just got everything that you really want a traditional – in the best sort of old-fashioned sense – leading man to have." The scene near the end where Van Helsing transforms from a werewolf back into his human self was originally shot with Hugh nude, but the director decided it would take away from the emotion of Anna's death because viewers would be distracted. (Uh, no comment.) So the final edit covered his behind with a CGI loin cloth.

While filming in Prague, Hugh studied tap dancing and singing to prepare for the upcoming musical. The amount of singing in *The Boy from Oz* would require a very relaxed and efficient technique to do 20 songs a night eight times a week for a year.

Hugh took a quick break from filming to host the Tony Awards for the first time on June 8, 2003. The producers asked him because of his upcoming starring role on Broadway, but I'm betting they also had seen footage of him hosting in Australia. On stage at Radio City Music Hall, Hugh shared that he had Peter Allen's old dressing room for the evening, "which makes this really the most extravagant and expensive piece of research ever staged." He said it was the most fun he'd ever had on stage up to that point and told Deb afterward, "I really hope they ask me to do it again one day!" (How about next year? And the year after that?)

After filming wrapped, the *Van Helsing* cast went to Comic-Con in July to promote the upcoming movie. The audience asked Hugh to sing, and his irrepressible "have a go" spirit took over, trying to get *Oklahoma!* co-star Shuler Hensley to join him in a chorus of "Poor Jud." Shuler didn't have Hugh's spontaneous showman spirit, so Hugh tried "Summer Lovin'" from *Grease.* Still no help. Hugh had to play both Danny and Sandy himself.

Toward the end of July they flew home to Australia where *Standing Room Only* was shown at the Melbourne International Film Festival. The message of the film is that the most extraordinary things in life often aren't made up of momentous experiences or big goals. The beauty in life is found in what happens along the way. "Life happens when you least expect it," Deb says.

And speaking of unexpected things happening along the way, what happens when an action movie star plays a flamboyant entertainer in a Broadway musical?

CHAPTER 6

NEW YORK, NEW YORK

In August of 2003, Hugh (with Deb and Oscar of course!) came to New York and started rehearsals for his Broadway debut. In a rehearsal open to the media, Hugh could hardly stand still in the background as he waited for his turn to come on stage. Even after hearing the music every day, it made him want to dance! One thing that took some getting used to about New York was driving. Legend has it Oscar's favorite word at age three was asshole, from spending time in the car with Deb at the wheel...

The first preview was on September 16, and the show officially opened on October 16. It started off a little slowly—critics didn't love it at first, but Hugh could tell audiences were connecting with it. Some reviewers did see the power. Rex Reed with the *New York Observer* wrote, "The new theater season exploded with *The Boy from Oz*. It is a sensational one man show business phenomenon called Hugh Jackman. I have never seen any male performer with so much passion, talent, energy, charisma, and panache in all the years I've been attending Broadway musicals." It would end up breaking 11 box office records.

A producer told Hugh that as a Broadway star, he should really have a solo album. *There's that annoying word: should.* So he signed with a record label and recorded a lot of songs. But he recalled, "I was in the studio because someone said I should do an album, not because I had anything to say — so it was terrible. I hated it." So he walked away from it. That takes a lot of wisdom to get that far into the process and pull the plug because it doesn't feel authentic. I admire that artistic integrity. *But in 2019 will we finally get a Hugh Jackman solo album?*

A strong indication of Hugh's acting talent were the persistent rumors about his sexuality as a result of playing Peter Allen. He inhabited Peter so fully and convincingly that audience members who weren't familiar with Hugh's family life came away believing what they had seen on stage. I can understand their confusion, because Hugh-as-Peter creates unbelievable heat on stage with both women and men in the space of a few minutes.

I'll let Carol Bayer Sager describe how his talent touched her. Carol worked closely with Peter, co-writing many of his best known songs, including the Oscar-winner, Arthur's Theme (also called "The Best That You Can Do," also known as the one about the moon and New York City).

When I gave him a hug after the first preview, I had to remember that I was hugging a man I don't know all that well, because I felt I was hugging a part of Peter. I almost feel teary [talking about it] because it gets confusing for me when I watch the show. He so brilliantly captured Peter, that I want Peter to be here.

Deb recalled how much fun it was for them to be the new kids in the Broadway community. She said Hugh "took the town by storm" and she enjoyed every minute of the ride. She herself saw the show 40-ish times. Hugh teased, "I think it's the only one of my shows you haven't fallen asleep in." (As Deb says, she has "two speeds: stop and go." So usually when she sits down in a dark theater...) And Deb had a little fun of her own with the gay rumors. She described that often in the ladies' room at intermission the "Is he or isn't he?" conversation would be buzzing. When she was in the mood, she'd call out from her bathroom stall, "He isn't!"

When Hugh talked about the show "bringing out different sides of me," I think every reporter was hoping for a coming out scoop. But Hugh was referring to allowing himself-as-Peter to be way more "naughty" and outrageous than he had ever been before. Likewise when he said playing Peter was "therapeutic" and that it had a "bigger reverberation in my life than any other show," interviewers waited with bated breath for what came next. But it was Peter's tug-of-war between the desire for stardom and his personal relationships that had Hugh thinking deeply about family. Allen's iconic "I Still Call Australia Home" contains the lyrics, "All the sons and daughters, spinning round the world, away from their family and friends..." Being in the US while his mother and sisters lived in

74

England and his father and brothers lived in Australia, those words hit home. Hugh reflected during the show's run:

> *Every night when I sing it, it kind of strikes me that on one level I'm the happiest I've ever been in my life – the dream of being here on Broadway. And at the same time I'm feeling very sentimental about my family and my relationships – my parents, and spending time with them, and evaluating what is really important.*

Hugh developed a habit of ad libbing with the audience for at least a few minutes in every performance. He loves that benefit of live theater where the performer and the audience can feed off each other's energy, and it can be a different experience every night. He connects with audiences in a way that not every actor can pull off. "You can't be a great improviser if you're not a great actor," said Isabel Keating, who played Judy Garland. She was reflecting on how Hugh always stayed in character no matter what surprises came at him from audience members, like the woman who yelled out, "I wanna bite your ass!" Thinking he was calling a bluff, he invited her to the stage. She wasn't bluffing, and it left a mark! Theater-goers loved his openness. Hugh recalled, "That show was rowdy. People were just going crazy. One woman saw the show 200 times!" They weren't only fanatical inside the theater, many people stopped him on the street to tell stories of their encounters with Peter. Quite a number of people proudly proclaimed that they'd slept with him! "And all I want to say is, 'You're not the only one, pal!' Girls, guys, everyone! I'd say that's happened at least 100 times."

During the run of *The Boy From Oz,* Hugh appeared on *Inside the Actors Studio* with James Lipton for the first time, with his proud wife and mother both in the audience. What eventually aired was about 40 minutes of career overview, but the uncut interview was four and a half hours long! In an interview with Charlie Rose he said he hoped to be doing some Shakespeare soon. That opportunity hasn't come to fruition yet, so it must still be on the vision board.

So what about people who said Hugh was crazy to take a break from his movie career to do a wildly different role on Broadway? Thanks to his following his gut, directors and casting agents got a whole new perspective of his acting range. His performance caught the attention of directors such as Woody Allen, Darren Aronofsky, and Christopher Nolan.

The producers of the Oscars also took note of his ability to keep an audience in the palm of his hand, and put him on their list as a potential host. His 2009 performance at the Oscars would lead directly to *The Greatest Showman.*

When something sounds like fun... it's your intuition speaking. Trust it!

Aronofsky came to see *The Boy From Oz* and loved it! He came backstage afterward, and during their conversation Hugh brought up *The Fountain*, a screenplay written by Darren. Brad Pitt had originally been booked to play the lead but that had fallen through. Hugh said he was intrigued by the story and asked if he could read the script. At first Darren said no, which Hugh took to mean that he'd been too forward in asking, but the next day Darren called and asked if Hugh really meant it. *(It's not uncommon that what appears to one person to be arrogance, is actually the other person's insecurity.)* When Hugh got the script that night, he was so drawn in by the message of hope and eternal connection, he read it all the way through, hardly noticing his usual post-performance exhaustion.

The next day Hugh called Darren and said he didn't want to assume that he would be offered the part, but that he would love to do it if Darren could wait until his Broadway commitment was finished. (Hugh didn't think of bringing his agent into the loop until *after* that conversation.) Darren agreed to wait for Hugh, which had ancillary benefits. Those months of Hugh being on stage every evening allowed them collaboration time during the day. They were able to more fully develop the character(s) Hugh would play: a single soul housed in three very different figures through time. Hugh had time do extra research, even meeting with neuroscientists and observing brain surgery in preparation for playing Tommy.

Also during *The Boy from Oz* run, *Van Helsing* opened in May of 2004, but Hugh limited publicity to what he could do in New York or by video or phone, so that he didn't miss performances. (His understudy complained that he never got to go on, and in fact, the few times during the year-long run that Hugh had scheduled time off, the show shut down rather than having Kevin Spirtas step in!) *Van Helsing* was number one at the box office on opening weekend, and earned Hugh nominations for Best Hero at the MTV Awards and Best Movie Actor at the Teen Choice Awards.

Hugh described the Monday morning after it opened to David Letterman.

I'm a bit like a teenager these days doing theater, I wake up a bit late. So I woke up about a quarter to nine to these screams from my living room. My wife ran in and said, 'You and the show got nominated for Tonys, and your movie has made 53 million dollars and it's number one!' I was like, 'I think I need to record that. This is something I should wake up to every morning.' When I'm sixty and watching reruns of Van Helsing and X-Men I'll be like, 'One day, kid, I used to...'

It's true! Part of the Joy Revolution is to focus on what's going right, because it energizes you!

That June Hugh hosted the Tony Awards again, this time keeping up with the Rockettes in the opening and riding on stage on a camel for his own *Boy from Oz* performance. (Interesting trivia: the camel was a descendant of the camel Peter Allen rode when he performed at Radio City Music Hall.) Standing backstage when Nicole Kidman read his name as the winner for Best Leading Actor in a Musical was quite an experience. "I've been up here all night and I am now absolutely trembling," he said. Then true to form, "I'm going to start with the most important, my wife. I love you. I couldn't have done this without you, and even if I could it certainly wouldn't have been as much fun as it is." Deb blew kisses back from the audience, overcome with emotion as well.

In addition to preparing for *The Fountain,* Hugh used his flexibility of time during the day to start work on voicing two animated features. On *Flushed Away* he was thrilled to be working with the team that made *Chicken Run!* But animation was more of a challenge than he expected. "It's very exacting because as an actor you get used to using your eyes and facial expressions, and even though your expressions are duplicated, you have to get so much across with your voice." On the other hand he found it freeing to act without worrying about a set or makeup or where the camera was. "One session I went in and only did screaming and yelling and reactions! Because Roddy falls from great heights all over the place." As a special nod to Hugh, one of the outfits Roddy considers while deciding what to wear is Wolverine-style yellow spandex. (Hugh didn't know about that until he saw the final film!) Roddy's musical tribute to his ally, Rita, was improvised in the moment. Hugh was shocked that was the take they used, but I suppose rats don't usually sound like polished Broadway performers.

While he was playing a James-Bond-style rat character, it made sense to also take on an Elvis-style penguin character, right? As Memphis in *Happy Feet,* Hugh sang "Heartbreak Hotel" to seduce his penguin mate, voiced by Nicole Kidman. He recalled having so much fun in the recording studio – dancing along while he sang – that he was sweating at the end.

By the time *The Boy From Oz* was scheduled to close, it had become hugely popular, and the producers begged Hugh to extend his contract for another three months. But Hugh was literally limping toward the finish line. There was so much dancing and jumping up and down from the top of the piano that Hugh had multiple stress fractures in his feet and had to ice them for hours every day to get through the shows. They considered a few other actors to take over the role (names like Harry Connick, Jr. and John Travolta were mentioned), but in the end they decided it didn't make sense to have anyone try to follow Hugh's performance. On closing night, as he sang the final "Once Before I Go," the roof almost came off the Imperial Theatre. Hugh had already said playing Van Helsing was physically tougher than Wolverine, but *The Boy From Oz* was far more difficult than either one. Following its close, they went back to Australia for some time off so Hugh's feet could heal.

Filming of *The Fountain* began in Montreal in December 2004. Deb and Oscar stayed in the apartment in New York instead of traveling with him because he knew it would be an emotionally intense, introspective role. He went home to them most weekends, though.

> *This was the first time I worked without my family being there, because we always travel together. But I said, 'Deb, I have a feeling with this one there's not going to be much left of me at the end of the day,' and there wasn't. I'd wake up in the morning and do yoga for an hour and half, and then work all day and then I'd collapse. I'd collapse at lunchtime often, but thrillingly so. It was an exhaustion that was really rewarding.*

Director Darren Aronofsky confirms that dedication. "Hugh is an exceptional actor and incredibly skillful technically... He was so willing to try things in every different way. We would run take after take and we would try every single emotion that could possibly work and throw out ideas to each other." *When people work together, each doing what they love, the dedication and creativity are off the charts.* On a lighter note, it's fun to hear Hugh's description of filming the sensual bathtub scene.

> *When we were shooting, Rachel [Weiss] and Darren were dating very seriously. The scene really didn't call for us to go too far – I fall in the bathtub, we start kissing, end of scene. Darren said, 'I just want to make it clear that you're about to make love.'*
>
> *So, 60 seconds into kissing, we're still not cutting... and then she pulls off my shirt, and she's naked, and we're still going... and then I hear 'Take his pants off!' I started laughing and said, 'Darren, this is just too kinky. I can't keep going.'*

Then the sense of humor that gives his publicist gray hairs kicks in.

> *That was the woman I'm making out with's boyfriend, five feet away. I mean, not since college had I been in that situation...*

The story set in the present was filmed first, then the past, and finally the part in the future. Hugh shaved his head for the last portion. In fact, he shaved his entire body, to help with feeling like a completely different physical being. The hours of yoga paid off; behind the scenes footage showed him with his nose to his knees warming up. And after Hugh performed an incredible sequence of climbing up the tree then flying above it on a wire, Aronofsky was overheard saying, "The fucked up thing is people are going to think it's a stunt man." On the last day of principal photography (February 24) Hugh said he was "exhausted in every way but very satisfied at the same time, which is kind of a thrilling feeling." He said he'd been pushed farther into vulnerability and openness and raw emotion than ever before as an actor. "At some point you have to just let go and go for the ride and enjoy it."

When you're doing what you were born to do, you can accomplish things you never thought were possible.

When filming was complete, the family headed to Australia for Deb's first major acting role since becoming a mom, in the movie *Jindabyne*. Hugh took over as primary parent, and I have to wonder what that transition was like. No matter how dedicated a parent you are, it's a huge contrast to go from hours of daily yoga and playing an intensely emotional and intellectual role, to spending all day every day with a preschooler. Hugh may actually be better at it than most people. He has said, "I feel like a little kid all the time."

It felt good to Deb to be using her creative talents on screen again, but there were times she was on location when she would think, "I don't want to be here. I want to be home with my family." *We all have a variety of things we love to do, and our priorities shift in different phases of life. The important thing is to be aware of how you're feeling so you can adjust your plans accordingly.* Her journey toward more directing was also continuing. The short film she had written and directed a few years previously, *Standing Room Only,* was released in February of 2005 on a compilation DVD called *Stories of Lost Souls.* Shortly after that, Hugh and Deb formed a production company together with a friend, called Seed Productions.

In June, Hugh hosted the Tony Awards for the third time in a row with his hair still growing back from filming *The Fountain.* He sang "Somewhere" with Aretha Franklin which remains one of my favorite musical moments. Then it was straight off to London to work with another iconic director, Woody Allen, filming *Scoop.* Compared to other films Hugh had done, he said that one almost felt like a vacation, getting off work mid-afternoon most days.

In July, they became a family of four when they adopted Ava. Five year old Oscar said, "I've waited my whole life for this." I haven't heard Hugh or Deb talk a lot about those first days of having two kids, but for me, it was the most overwhelming stage of life. Trying to run a business while being home with a toddler and an infant was A LOT. *If you're in this situation right now, let go of any shoulds, mamas! Your goal is that the kids are alive at the end of the day and you know where they are. Big bonus points if you've showered.*

Their newly expanded family soon headed to Vancouver for the filming of Hugh's third Wolverine movie, *X-Men: The Last Stand.* Brett Ratner's goal as the director was to keep the good things that had happened in the first two, but to make this one funnier, sexier, and more emotional. Hugh's only regret was "I think we got slightly carried away with the hairspray." He also found working with Kelsey Grammer to be a bit "problematic," because "there is more footage on the cutting room floor of me laughing..."

Richard Bradshaw, Hugh's brother-in-law, once again acted as his stunt double. Richard speaks very highly of Hugh, that he's "an amazing athlete and up for learning pretty much anything from fights to high falls, spinning cars to cattle wrangling. He's the greatest pupil and learns so fast, but will happily step aside if he understands there is too much of a potential for danger, not letting his ego get in the way of the process of making cool action. The ideal combination in an actor." It's nice that they admire each other; that must make family holidays easier. And Hugh did enjoy doing as much as he could himself, including that huge backflip out of the tree.

Hugh took a short break from filming to attend the Emmy Awards in September where he won for hosting the 2004 Tony Awards. As Hugh said, "Only in America can you win an award for hosting an award show." In October, he signed on to *The Prestige* with Christopher Nolan as his next project. What attracted him to that role? "No one with any sense would say no to Christopher Nolan."

Filming for *X-Men 3* continued through January, then there was hardly any break at all before filming of *The Prestige* started. But at least they got to move from Vancouver, which is pretty frigid filming outdoors in the middle of the night in January, to Los Angeles. I'm not sure when Hugh found time to do research for this role, but he has quite a story about Nolan encouraging him to go see David Copperfield's show in Las Vegas and meet with him afterward (as told to *Indie London*):

> *[David took us] to this street on the outskirts of Vegas, to this sex shop! I was with my wife so there were the three of us, at a sex shop, and he pulls out his keys and opens the door. We walked in and I'm thinking "Alright what have we got into here?"*
>
> *Then he says: "Push the nipple on the mannequin over there." I pushed the nipple and these doors open and you enter this museum, the size of four football fields, of magic memorabilia. It was 12:30 at night and he did a 90 minute show for us, until two in the morning. He showed me exactly how Houdini got out of his water escape thing and how old tricks were done. But he's the consummate showman and there's no revealing [his own] secrets whatsoever.*

A major piece of preparation Hugh did was writing his character's diary (which was then used in filming) from age 18 through the age he was in the story. That's some intense background work. Hugh was quite honored to be working closely with Michael Caine, and completely star struck meeting David Bowie, which turned into Episode 2 of What Not To Do When You Meet Your Heroes. He told Bowie the story about when he got tickets to his 1981 Australia tour (Hugh was in middle school) but ended up selling the ticket to a friend who offered him more money. Awkward silence. Bowie called him "the scalper" the rest of their time together on set.

Wednesdays were kids days on set. Christian Bale's daughter was close in age to Ava, although playdates for 8-month-olds are pretty limited in scope, I suppose. Hugh hoped he would learn some magic tricks to impress his kids and their friends, but either Oscar was a pretty tough audience or Hugh was a pretty bad magician. "The very first trick I had to do involved a flower that I had to make disappear. I was working on it for a while and practiced on my son the night before filming – he was five at the time – and he said, 'Daddy, it's in your other hand.' It didn't bode well for filming, and it's been cut from the movie."

Hugh actually played two roles in *The Prestige*: Robert Angier and Angier's double, for which he wore a slight prosthetic nose piece, prosthetic earlobes, and fake teeth. People still argue with each other (and even with him!) over whether or not he actually played both parts. "It was one of those rare opportunities for me who has done some theater to be able to, while filming, get up on the stage. I think there were a few calls from behind the camera of 'Stop doing that, you old ham!' but I was having a good time." The producers were delighted! Aaron Ryder said, "These guys love their roles. They bring it every day and it shows ultimately in their work." Perhaps the only thing Hugh didn't enjoy about that project was working with doves. Evidently working with live animals wasn't covered in acting school.

In February, Hugh made a quick visit to Australia to do some advance press for *The Boy from Oz* arena show. A trip home, especially with a little ocean time, always seems to make Hugh's smile just a little brighter. He told Richard Wilkins of the Today show, "I was kayaking in the harbor this morning" with his old friend Michael Ryan, a trainer from the gym he had worked in prior to attending WAAPA. Filming of *The Prestige* finished in early April, then the family had a little bit of time to catch their breath.

It's dizzying to see the schedule for press around the world when a major movie opens. Hugh and Halle Berry were in Mexico City for the premiere of *X-Men: The Last Stand* on May 15, then to the UK the next day, taping an appearance on the *Jonathan Ross Show* among other things. Deb got to join in the fun at the Cannes Film Festival, because both *X3* and *Jindabyne* premiered there! That was quite an adventure for them both to be promoting movies at the same time. They stayed in the Sean Connery suite at the Carlton Hotel, which had a little private elevator straight down to the bar. Hugh's movie premiered on May 22, Deb's on May 23.

Back in New York, Hugh did more press in advance of the US premiere on May 26. In an interview with Martha Stewart, they talked about how crazy it was that this was the first of SIX movies he had coming out that year, including the two animated features. He mentioned that the press tour had taken him away from the kids for nine days, so that meant 10-month-old Ava was "practically driving" when he returned.

But Deb reinforced that life wasn't all travel and glamour. "We are just a family going along. When we go to do the red carpet, it is the job, like going to Disneyland for the day. It is not really our life. We are at home changing diapers and going to the supermarket." They didn't have a permanent home at that point, home was wherever one of them was working at the time. But with Oscar getting to school age, they were looking for a home base, and New York was the most likely prospect. I'm pretty sure Deb had been clear about that from the beginning, telling Hugh while they were dating that she loved New York and intended to live there. Part of their goal in starting their own production company was to have more control over where projects were filmed, making it easier for the kids to put down roots.

Oprah visited the Jackmans at home for an article in *Oprah* magazine. She described almost-1-year-old Ava lighting up as Deb handed her to Hugh when he came in the door, and 6-year-old Oscar scampering in and grabbing Hugh's leg. It was 100% clear to her that family was Hugh's first priority.

In June, Hugh committed to the unnamed-at-that-point big romantic epic with director Baz Luhrman which would shoot the following year in Australia. Heath Ledger was originally attached to play the role of Drover, but backed out for *The Dark Knight.* Russell Crowe was asked next, but he eventually turned it down and suggested Hugh. Hugh joked, "I've been coming off the bench for Russell Crowe my entire career." *Whatever works! Accept opportunities from any direction!*

More world travel for *X3* followed, mixed in around rehearsals for *The Boy from Oz* arena tour. The Korean premiere was in Seoul on June 14, the Chinese premiere at the Shanghai International Film Festival was on June

19, and the Japanese premiere was in Tokyo on July 13. *Remember that little boy with a map of the world on his wall?*

Jindabyne premiered in Australia on July 16th, so Hugh got to be Deb's "corporate husband" that night. She was nominated for an Australian Film Institute Best Supporting Actress award and won a Film Critics Circle of Australia award. The following week, *Scoop* was released and the week after that the Australian tour of *The Boy from Oz* arena show began.

Do you get tired just reading this? It's such a great point about how to live the Joy Revolution – when you look at something that isn't your personal strength, it looks exhausting. But when you're truly doing what you love, it energizes you! We all have days when we're drained, no matter what, but take a look at your overall picture. Do you have more days when you're tired or more days when you're energized? If it's the former, it's time to change something up. Go back and read Chapter 2 again. Because the world needs the variety of what we all love for life to be a rich, full experience. It needs people like Hugh with boundless energy for performing, and people like me who would rather spend Christmas vacation researching and writing a book.

Did Hugh find it exhausting? Quite the opposite. "The stars are aligning for me," he said. He was working with several amazing directors in a row, playing a role he loved in front of huge crowds in his home country, and getting to be a husband and father every night.

Hugh and company did 42 shows in different cities across Australia in six weeks. They added in songs like "My Pretty Keen Teen" that were in the original musical book but not part of the Broadway version. My guess is Hugh went for the arena experience simply because it sounded like a blast! "Bigger than the show's ever been before, do everything as big as we can," is how he described their plan. Could he make 16,000 people each feel like the most important person in the room? Like they were part of something huge and also very intimate? "I don't think I've ever been as excited about something as I am about this show," he said during preparation. And how did it feel performing in front of tens of thousands of screaming fans? "All my rock star dreams are coming true."

Audiences and reviewers responded. Martin Ball reported, "What began life eight years ago as a musical has now become an arena spectacular, and while Allen and his songs are the ostensible reason, this is really The Hugh Jackman Show. There is no set to speak of, and the story has been stripped back, but in many ways the show has found a natural form, since it lets Jackman revel in showmanship, just as Allen himself did." He later added, "Jackman is clearly having a great time, especially in his banter with the audience." Sometimes Hugh had so much fun ad libbing in character he would crack himself up! And when the snorts would start, the cast surrounding him would lose it, too! At one show he reached into the audience to give some high fives and found himself pulled off the stage, dragged into a "mosh pit of senior citizens. I got groped a lot!" Security!

While Hugh was on tour, Deb traveled with him some of the time, but she also focused on opening an Australian office of their production company. "We are committed to putting back into the industry here, to create work, build bridges and develop synergies between Australia and the US," she said. Both *Jindabyne* and *The Fountain* were shown at the Toronto International Film Festival in September, but Deb and Hugh were still in Australia, wrapping up the arena spectacular.

What about their production company back in Los Angeles? The development of a Wolverine spin-off wasn't going according to plan, but when they returned from Australia, production started on the first feature film Hugh and Deb produced, *Deception*. It was also director Marcel Langenegger's first feature film. He had previously directed commercials. (A few years later Hugh would again recruit a director from commercials into making his first feature film: Michael Gracey on *The Greatest Showman*.) *Deception* is a bizarre little film with lots of twists and turns but an unfortunately disappointing ending. After all the intrigue, it wraps up kind of like a Disney movie where the villain dies and the hero and heroine ride off into the sunset (ok, not literally). Or maybe I just don't like seeing Hugh die on screen. (Sorry. Spoiler.) The alternate ending in the DVD extras is stronger, in my humble opinion.

They filmed *Deception* mostly in New York City and some in Madrid. An interviewer asked why Ewan McGregor got almost all the sex scenes. Hugh's response with a smile was, "Did you see that my wife is co-producer?" Mr. Over-Sharer tells a funny story about Ewan. Several of his liaison scenes were filmed on the same day, and at lunchtime he called his wife and said, "Get on a plane. You need to be here by tonight." On a tamer note, Ewan plays the guitar and loves to sing as much as Hugh, so there was a lot of music on set between takes.

Deb also filmed *Sleepwalking* in Canada in October, all while another whirlwind of press was getting started for the release of FOUR different movies. Still in October there were appearances and galas and the premiere of *The Prestige* in Los Angeles and of *Flushed Away* in New York.

At the latter, Hugh and Kate Winslet got to slide down a huge inflatable "toilet" slide. November brought premieres of *The Prestige* in London and Paris, of *The Fountain* in Los Angeles and New York, and of *Flushed Away* in London, Berlin, and Rome. I think Deb and the kids went along for most if not all of it!

Mixed in between were lots and lots of press interviews. How he remembered his own name is beyond me, let alone which movie and which colleagues he was answering questions about on any given day. *Happy Feet* had its premiere during that time as well, but I don't know how Hugh would have fit one more thing in!

What a year! I have to say he did look a little tired in some of the press videos. It's a good thing they enjoy traveling. Deb says that wherever the four of them are together is home. She used scents like eucalyptus to establish each new spot as immediately feeling like home for the kids. They spent a few days in Egypt at Oscar's request. Since Hugh worked on Thanksgiving Day, the studio said the family could take the jet anywhere they wanted in Europe for the rest of the weekend. (Europe... Egypt... close enough.)

A key benefit of doing the animated shows was being able to share his work with the kids. About *Flushed Away*, he said: "When I was in the theatre with my son, sitting next to him, the look in his face... He said to me afterwards: 'This is my favorite movie ever.' He can't stop talking about it. When he was watching it, he couldn't stop looking at me, and it was one of the great moments for me in the business."

Whether all the films were box office hits or not, Hugh was in his element expanding his limits as an actor, feeling thoroughly satisfied artistically. About *The Prestige* he said, "Look, I was in the movie, and I've seen it three times, and on the third watching I went 'Ah! That!' There are so many twists and turns and so many subtle details, you don't want to miss a frame." About *The Fountain:* "As an actor, it was the most challenging thing I'd ever read. Emotionally it's very extreme. I'd be blessed if I got to play these three roles in three separate films. But to get to play them all in one film was an amazing opportunity."

2007 brought a little breathing room, as Hugh focused on preparing for his role in *Australia.* That preparation involved a lot of horseback riding, since a drover needs to be an expert horseman. He did some training in Texas and some in upstate New York.

Then they headed back "home" to Australia for the filming of two big movies. *Australia* was filmed partly in Sydney and partly on location in the outback. They filmed for a total of nine months (only three days shorter than *Titanic* in fact). Starting in Sydney, they shot the scenes at the ball, where a clean-shaven Drover shows up in a very Clark-Gable-looking white suit jacket to accept Lady Ashley's invitation to dance. Deb was on set that day to enjoy the fun. "Wear that costume home tonight," she requested. Stimulates the imagination, doesn't it?

During the time on location in the outback, they had the option to drive back to the closest city every night, but that was an hour and a half each way, and Hugh figured he would much rather stay on the set to have more downtime and enjoy the quiet remoteness. So he lived in his trailer for six weeks, and for most of that time Oscar stayed there with him (Deb and Ava visited on weekends). He told about seeing Oscar at the campfire in the early morning learning from David Gulpilil, the renowned Aboriginal actor, how to clean and cook catfish over a fire.

Hugh took a lot of grief from the crew about the famous shower-by-the-campfire scene. He came back from lunch that day and all the crew had their shirts off, had oiled up their torsos, and exaggerated their movements all afternoon. Filming with horses and cattle (and flies!) in the elements wasn't easy. "I actually fainted once, fell off the horse I can't tell you how many times, and we had some pretty hairy situations, but it was also amazing. Because we were in parts of the country that you would never go to in your life." It was Hugh's first film back home after spending eight years in Hollywood and he was thrilled to be able to use his own accent again.

Deb continued to work in their production company and in mid-May a TV series called *Viva Laughlin* was greenlit for 13 episodes. It was a bit of a stretch as an idea, a casino cop thriller that also happened to be a musical. Hugh co-produced and guest-starred as a rival casino owner. The pilot aired on October 18th. The official season premiere aired on October 21st. And the show was canceled on October 22nd.

I love Deb's perspective on that experience. "Doing a drama that is a musical is going to be a huge risk," she said. "If I'm going to fail, I want to fail spectacularly, and it seems like we did." *That's right! Go big or go home!* Hugh's comment on their future in producing was "We'll keep trying, doing things that we are passionate about and curious about." *Yes!* And it's a testament to their vision that when the idea was floated only two years later of an original musical based on P.T. Barnum's life, they didn't run screaming, but embraced the idea!

Being back in Australia, Hugh and Deb were getting a lot of questions about how they had adopted their children. People would say, "We would love to adopt, but it's just so hard!" Deb started asking, "Why is it so hard? What can we do about it?" Deb read a story in the newspaper about a woman who adopted a child in China but couldn't get approval to bring her child back to Australia. Deb called the paper to share her perspective about how many Australian families wanted to adopt but it was too hard. The next thing she knew, she was pictured on the front page of the newspaper with an editorial saying they wanted to support her and her "action lobby group." She looked around saying "Uh, and where might they be?"

Because of their celebrity status, press requests immediately started coming in to interview Deb about her (unintended) activism around adoption, and before long she was asked to speak to Australian government officials in Canberra. Deb felt incredibly intimidated, but she also had the sense that she had a chance to make a real difference. So she invited a group of experts in child advocacy over for dinner, saying she had a forum to speak out and wanted them to educate her so that she could take the right action. What a beautiful example of a powerful way to use fame. That led to her starting National Adoption Awareness Week.

Let's talk about fear and courage. What is courage, and can it be taught? Can you acquire it when you're not feeling it? What factors enabled Deb to step up in such a big way? It really goes back to the balance between the Want Engines and Belief Engines in your brain. Deb has a deep and profound passion for children (clarity and power of Want). She also had a strong foundation of self-confidence in other areas (a starting place for Belief in a new endeavor), and she took the time to educate herself on the topic (preparation increases belief in yourself). In addition, she had people she trusted cheering her on (excellent fuel for your Belief Engines). That's a great recipe for doing big things!

The final month or so of filming *Australia* got a little more complicated as morning sickness hit Nicole. But they got it wrapped in December and had about a month to enjoy the holidays before the filming of *X-Men Origins: Wolverine* began in the middle of January. It was filmed primarily in Australia and New Zealand.

Hugh had a blast working with Liev Schreiber again. The competitiveness they share spurred them on during stunts and fight scenes. There is hilarious behind the scenes footage of them practicing their fight choreography being extremely careful not to mess up Hugh's hair! Hugh took his physical preparation to another level again, and was really pleased with the primal look he was able to achieve coming up out of the tank, with no computer enhancement. He spent three full days in – and coming out of – that water tank, by the way. He said they were three pretty uncomfortable days. He couldn't hear anything under water, so the director gave him cues by pulling on his toes. Evidently Gavin got overly enthusiastic a few times. Those poor toes.

Liev was originally given a muscle suit to look comparable to Hugh, but decided instead to see if he could sufficiently bulk up. When Hugh taught him the amount of protein it requires, Liev called it the "genocide of chickens." He also reflected, "We're both rounding 40 and here we are doing this young man's job, and neither one of us wanted to admit that all we wanted to do was go home and get in an Epsom salt bath."

*Let's pause a minute. Did Hugh work hard physically playing Wolverine? Incredibly hard. So this is a good time for a reminder that the Joy Revolution doesn't mean only doing easy things or lowering your expectations. Here's the key part: **Hugh wanted** to see how far he could go—to achieve an effect that matched the character he felt. No one was putting that external expectation on him. When you're doing what you love, your internal drive is incredibly strong. It's a bit ironic to me that Hugh receives less credit in the acting world for the actual physical transformation of his body than actors who subject themselves to dramatic costume and makeup effects. But inexplicably, awards voters haven't yet asked my opinion.*

Lynn Collins, who played Kayla Silverfox, was thrilled to work with Hugh, having been especially impressed with his performance in *The Fountain.* "When I was told I got the job I was incredibly nervous, then in 72 hours I was on top of a cliff in New Zealand in my underwear making out with Hugh Jackman." That's a good day at work.

Troye Sivan was on set just for a couple weeks playing Wolverine's younger self, and Hugh was very supportive and encouraging with the child actor. I'll let Troye describe it:

> *I had never acted before, this was my first ever audition, and I really got dropped into this fantasy for two weeks. He was so lovely and so generous. I remember he came up to me after a day of filming and said, 'I'm about to go film something on a green screen, do you want to come watch?' so I watched him do some cool motorbike tricks in front of a*

green screen. As a fan of the X-Men series, or any 12-year-old boy around the world, it was the coolest thing.

Deception was released in April but Hugh did most of his publicity for that film remotely. Hearing him reflect on the producer role, it sounded to me as if it didn't bring him nearly as much joy as acting. He referred to producing as "heavy lifting" and "a lot of detail." But he really "relished the moments" in front of the camera. He had similar things to say about producing the first Wolverine movie. "Being an actor is like being a little kid all the time. That's the challenge is to stay open and creative and playful. Being a producer is like being an uber-grownup all the time."

Pssst, this is your higher self talking. Focus on what you love to do. Other people love to do the producing part but could never do the literal heavy lifting you do to prepare for a role!

In April, Hugh was a delegate to the prime minister's Australia 2020 Summit sharing ideas for the country's future. At one of the after hours events, Hugh asked a young man who looked like a waiter to bring him a drink. Turns out it was Young Australian of the Year Hugh Evans, and the two of them talked for several hours that night about Hugh (E)'s goal to end extreme poverty around the globe by 2030. Hugh (J) and Deb were on board and helped Hugh (E) start what would become Global Citizen.

At the end of May Hugh received an alumni award from the University of Technology Sydney (where he got his journalism degree and took that one acting course that changed the trajectory of his life). That occasion was an opportunity to look back and reflect, and Hugh commented that his life felt "very much like a puzzle. There was no real plan, and it has kind of fit together in an odd way."

And that is really the best life plan of all. Pursue what you're passionate about, what you're drawn to. Dream big dreams, then follow your gut along the way.

When Hugh wrapped up the filming of *Origins*, Deb began filming *Beautiful* in South Australia. At the end of July, Hugh was a surprise guest at Comic-Con in San Diego to tease *Origins,* and said he had just gotten off a plane from Australia. He had grown back his Drover beard because they were getting ready to do some reshoots.

Later in 2008, Hugh and Deb visited Cambodia with World Vision. That trip cemented Deb's desire to do something about all the kids in the world without permanent families. Deb also filmed the movie *Blessed* in Melbourne, but while they were living and working in Australia they were searching for their permanent home in New York. They fell in love with a three story condo overlooking the Hudson River in Manhattan. That was a pretty nice 40th birthday present for Hugh.

At last they would be true New Yorkers.

CHAPTER 7

MAKING 40 LOOK DAMN GOOD

Some people dread turning 40. But I think it's safe to say Hugh was loving life. He and Deb had just spent a few years primarily back home in Australia taking turns filming movies. There were all the normal adventures of having small children (like making up games to get them to take baths), they were purchasing a permanent home in New York, his Rhett-Butler-like role was about to hit the big screen, he was about to be asked to host the Oscars, and he was about to be named *People's* Sexiest Man Alive.

Not a bad run.

Australia premiered in Sydney on November 18, then they flew to New York the next day to move into their new home. The day they arrived, Hugh was awarded one of the world's best-known titles: Sexiest Man Alive. How did that feel? Well, if you're Australian... Here's how he described it to Jay Leno the next day:

> The best thing about this announcement was I landed in America the day it came out and I wasn't in Australia. Because let me tell you, there's no end of hell. I mean, the concept of hazing, you have no idea. This morning I had probably 100 emails, 30 of which were from here, 'Congratulations!' and 70 of which I just didn't even bother opening. The nicest ones were like 'You've got to be kidding me, I've got tennis rackets sexier than you!' That's my best friend, and then it went more expletive from there.

Overall his response was "When you turn 40, to get something like that is better than a kick in the teeth, isn't it?" In the extensive interview with *People,* Hugh shared the names of his first girlfriend, first kiss, etc. That gave news crews an excuse to track down those women and ask them about their "intimate" history with Hugh. Oops, he felt bad about that in retrospect.

Another movie release, another whirlwind of premieres and press. The New York premiere of *Australia* was on November 24, Paris on December 1, Madrid on December 2, Rome on December 4, and London on December 10. Hugh talks about how acting requires being present in each moment, and I think doing press interviews all day long has to be the same. Being charming and fresh while answering the same questions over and over... It's easy to see why Hugh gets so excited when a journalist does something a little out of the ordinary, such as giving him a tray of traditional Australian food to explain. Hugh dove right in, tasting and describing them all, even being honest about the one that wasn't very good.

While Hugh was in London, he got the call from Steven Spielberg asking him to host the Oscars. It was 1:00 in the morning London time, so he doesn't remember exactly what he said, but he thinks it was something like "Yeah, I'll give it a go." When Deb walked in the room and asked why he looked so shocked, he said "Babe, you're about to get into bed with the host of the 81st Academy Awards!" Ever the quick wit, Deb said, "Billy Crystal's here??" But her teasing was short-lived, and she was so excited for him she was jumping up and down on the bed!

On December 13 Hugh and Nicole Kidman appeared on the German TV show "Wetten, dass...?" along with German Family Minister Ursula von der Leyen. She was delighted to "sit next to the sexiest man alive!" Hugh made a her (and more than a few audience members) swoon when he gallantly picked her up from inside the recycling bin where she had been doing a skit and carried her back to the couch on the stage.

Right after the holidays Hugh jumped into preparing for the Academy Awards, while still finding time to explore their new neighborhood and play in the snow with the kids. The Oscars would involve two huge song and dance numbers in addition to all the commentary. There was the fancy top-hat-and-tails duet with Beyonce, directed by Baz Luhrman, and then there was the question of what to do for the opening.

You know how entrepreneurs need to have a clear elevator speech? As in, can you explain your vision in 30 seconds? The story of how the opening number came to be is the most classic "elevator pitch" story ever.

Writers Dan Harmon and Rob Schrab had been tasked with coming up with ideas for Hugh in a way that was sensitive to the economic pressure everyone was feeling at the time. Dan described how Rob came up with the concept: "Why don't we have Hugh be this Boy Scout song-and-dance man, and in order to save money, he'd build it all himself, put it all together with cardboard and hot glue?" So they went for a production meeting, and fate smiled on them when Hugh got in the same elevator. In the time it took them to reach their floor, Hugh was eagerly on board with their plan and helped sell it to everyone else. As Dan said, "No one can say no to him when he's that enthusiastic."

The elevator pitch is real, folks. That level of clarity on what you have to offer is POWERFUL.

As it turned out, the third writer, Ben Schwartz, had been thinking of a similar idea even before they met, of Hugh portraying a guy who could pull off big entertainment value on almost no budget. (I'm so glad *Vulture* went back to these writers to get the scoop on how that magical piece came together!) The video of that opening number is an immediate Joy Bringer for me, no matter how many times I've seen it. The self-deprecating joke at the beginning about the Academy loving to "salute range" was Hugh's idea. The irony is pretty thick, I'd say, considering the extreme range Hugh had already displayed. Nineteenth century English duke, bisexual Australian entertainer, grumpy Canadian superhero, New York playboy, 26th century scientist, obsessive magician... Come on.

Once the idea was approved, Rob literally built the set pieces himself. Yes, there was hot glue involved. And because the other musical number was taking up so much rehearsal time, they only ever got to do one full rehearsal of the opening with all the technical aspects! Talk about pressure! Hugh's reflection was very real:

> *I always used to say to myself, 'I'm glad I do what I do.' Imagine being a 100 meter runner in the Olympics. Everything has to be perfect on that day. And I suppose in show biz, this is about as close as it'll come because there will never be so many people watching something I do at one time. Ever, no matter what I do.*

How does he handle that kind of intensity? First, he loves it. (Not everyone does, and we all get to pick!) In his case, "I need to drill it because I'm not a dancer, so I need to drill, drill, drill so that I can enjoy it." His acting teacher told him the same thing one of my mentors says – the emotions of "nervous" and "excited" feel the same in your body, so decide that what you're feeling is excitement! He goes on, "I never in my wildest dreams thought I'd be invited let alone host the bloody thing, so I'm determined to enjoy it."

Isn't that powerful? Say yes to things that give you a thrill, then do whatever preparation is needed to be able to enjoy the experience!

So does he ever have freak out moments? Oh yeah. He tells how he meditated as part of his preparation for the evening, set his intention to have fun above all, felt fantastic, then saw Meryl Streep in the front row from his vantage point backstage and reality came crashing down. When he heard the one minute call, Hugh was pretty sure he was going to throw up. At 15 seconds, the stage manager gave him a wink and said, "Good luck out there, only about a billion people watching!" And that made Hugh laugh. Thank goodness. As he walked out he was smiling, and he proceeded to knock everyone's socks off and have a ball doing it.

Our brains work so much better when we're laughing!

Hugh did have a great time, and that meant the audience did, too. In commercial breaks he interacted with the audience unscripted, throwing candy and being his goofball self. He comes alive on stage in a way few people can match. As one commentator put it, "The reason Jackman was so good was he made it a SHOW." The stage is his favorite place to be – singing, dancing, **connecting** with people. The writers of the opening number ended up winning an Emmy. Of course part of the credit goes to Hugh for how he sold it!

Whew! Did he take a vacation after that? Nope, he was back on the publicity circuit for *Australia* with a premiere in Japan four days later. Legend has it that trip included some karaoke with Hugh, Baz Luhrman, and Robert Pattinson dressed as Japanese schoolgirls. Or maybe only Baz and Hugh were dressed up, but they all sang. I haven't found any photographic evidence, but it certainly sounds like something our favorite goofball would do.

While rehearsing for the Academy Awards, Hugh had discovered he and David Rockwell, who was designing the sets for the show, had a mutual interest in Houdini. David shared that he'd been exploring the idea of creating a Broadway musical based on Houdini's life, and Hugh said he was in, both to support the project financially and to play the lead.

Two weeks later, producer Laurence Mark also came to Hugh with an idea – an original movie musical about the life of P.T. Barnum. A script had been written, they would just need the music. While they had boldly proclaimed "the musical is back!" in the Oscars number, an original movie musical was still a long shot project. It had been over 17 years since the last one had come out: *Newsies*. But it was just a crazy enough idea that it was fitting for a story about Barnum! Hugh said he was interested.

After a short break to continue settling into their New York home, it was time to ramp up publicity for *X-Men Origins: Wolverine*. The first showing was in front of a hometown crowd in Sydney on April 9, then on to Seoul on the 10th and Moscow on the 13th, where Hugh sang tunes by Sting and the Rolling Stones on a Russian talk show. Wolverine sings, people. Deal with it. Off-screen Hugh is who he is. And on around the world they went, to Rome, Madrid, London, Paris, and Berlin in the next five days.

Their first stop in the US was Grauman's Chinese Theatre in Hollywood on April 21 for Hugh to add his cement handprints and footprints to the collection there. *Another piece of the vision board coming true.* The kids didn't go to many public events, but Deb wanted them to be at that one since it was such a big milestone. When the three of them joined Hugh for a family photo after the ceremony, both kids desperately wanted to be held by their dad! He tried one on his back and one in his arms but that didn't work for the cameras. The next day they celebrated with a trip to Disneyland.

It was Hugh's idea to hold an online voting contest to see where the April 27 US premiere would be held, and Tempe, Arizona won! Roughly a thousand fans camped out for three days to get tickets, then 800 of them camped out again to get the best seats. When Hugh learned that, he ordered breakfast to be delivered for all 800. (I know, right?) When Hugh arrived at the premiere on a motorcycle, the sound was deafening (the crowd, not the motorcycle). The mayor of Tempe (also named Hugh) presented him with Wolverine Parking Only rights anywhere in the city. Nice perk!

Although Hugh was very upbeat during the press tour, he would later acknowledge that he wasn't altogether happy with the movie. It got too complicated, included way too many characters, and focused too much on action, not enough on the humanity of the mutants. He was already clear that the story he wanted to do next was the Samurai saga set in Japan. At the Japanese premiere, he invited all the attendees to audition!

It's so powerful that instead of spending energy bemoaning what didn't go exactly as he would have wished, he used the experience to clarify what he wanted next time. You can't go back anyway, so your power is in focusing forward.

Finally that summer Hugh got some down time. He mixed in some fun things like recording a Word of the Day segment on Sesame Street (Concentrate!) and singing onstage with Richard Marx. He perhaps didn't do his usual level of preparation for that performance as he kind of mangled the lyrics. His sheepish grin makes up for a lot though! Hugh was considering another comedy role as the lead in *Avon Man,* which they would also produce. In August he accepted a Teen Choice award for Choice Movie Actor: Action Adventure.

One of their adventures that summer had a bigger reverberation in their life than they ever imagined. They were invited by World Vision to visit Ethiopia to get a first-hand look at a community development program they had been supporting. They saw the human impact of buying fair trade coffee, and of offering support not just in crisis, but giving knowledge and technology so local farmers could become self-supporting – a "hand up, not just a hand out." Hugh said he wanted to experience what life was like for the coffee farmers, so he spent a day working with a young man named Dukale. Hugh is in pretty good shape (understatement), but the work was hard. And dirty. But what struck him most was that Dukale was smiling all day. And what did Dukale think? He was impressed. "For a person of such status, he was actually a very hard working farmer." It says something pretty cool about Hugh's character that when he told about having manure all over his hands and boots, he was smiling. As they left, Hugh told Dukale if there was any way he could help their community further, he would do it.

After working on the farm, Hugh accompanied the co-op's coffee broker to the commodities exchange. You can see in Hugh's eyes (in the documentary *Dukale's Dream)* how fascinated he was by the whole process. Back in New York, Hugh started asking every coffee seller he could find if they bought fair trade, and in many cases, he would explain the difference when they weren't familiar. "Meeting Dukale was in the middle of a very busy part of my life, and it totally stopped me in my tracks and made me reassess everything that I was doing in my life and why I was doing it and what is really important." The wheels were turning on the idea that would become Laughing Man Coffee. In September Hugh spoke to the United Nations kicking off Climate Week NYC. He shared what he'd witnessed first-hand—how the most vulnerable nations are the hardest hit by the effects of climate change.

And then Hugh was back on a Broadway stage, almost exactly five years from when *The Boy from Oz* closed. The producers of *A Steady Rain* had asked if he would do the play with Daniel Craig in London, but Hugh said with his kids in school in New York he couldn't be away from the family for that long. A day later they called back and asked if he would do it if it were on Broadway instead, and his answer was an immediate yes! For all the success Hugh had found in his acting career, this was significant because it was his first time doing what he had thought would be the bulk of his career – acting on stage in a play (vs. a musical). It was quite a theatrical challenge: two actors and two chairs, that's it. As part of their preparation for the roles, Daniel and Hugh spent some time with members of the Chicago Police. Can you imagine those cops showing up to work and being told their assignment for the day was to show James Bond and Wolverine around? The first place they took them was the morgue.

The show ran September 10 through December 6, and in November, Hugh signed on to film *Real Steel* the following summer (while the kids were off school). Also during this time Hugh filmed his bizarre little scene with Kate Winslet for the Farrelly brothers' project, *Movie 43*. They were the first two stars to sign on to the film, and their involvement convinced a lot of others to follow suit. (If you're not familiar, search online to find their scene. I won't spoil the surprise.) *When you're following what sounds fun, you win some and you lose some. But at least you had fun along the way!* How could Hugh know the final product would be released right after his first Academy Award nomination was announced? The universe has a sense of humor. And just as he had during his first Broadway run, Hugh again took advantage of his daytime availability to start work on voicing another animated feature—this time as the Easter Bunny in *Rise of the Guardians.*

In early 2010, after collecting the People's Choice Award for Favorite Action Star (and joking about running for governor of California), Hugh took his singing and dancing self to Brazil to film his first global TV ad role—a set of "Drink Positive" ads for Lipton Iced Tea. Lipton selected him based on his performance at the Oscars. "He is very different from many other actors. He is a true entertainer who can dance, sing and act. We will use all of his skills," their marketing director said. Hugh liked the campaign's focus on positivity and health. There were two directors being considered for the commercial shoot. One was French and the other, Michael Gracey, was Australian. The agency assumed Michael would know Hugh (don't all Australians know each other?) so they chose him. Divine intervention for sure.

Hugh loved working with Gracey, and said at the end of the shoot, "We should do a movie together!" Michael didn't get too excited since he'd heard the same thing from many stars he'd worked with over the years but nothing had ever come of it. **A couple weeks later Hugh sent Michael the first draft of the Barnum script**. It was Gracey's suggestion that they do a fantasy style musical with modern dancing and pop-sounding music, to make full use of Hugh's talents. **Michael's vision became so clear so quickly that he developed a pitch complete with concept art for most of the scenes**. *And they're pretty close to how the final product looked eight years later!* That vision turned into a long, labor-intensive development process, but aren't you glad these two guys kept focused on the magic they saw in their heads? Michael said "There's a Walt Disney quote, 'Make it so good, they have to want it,' and that became our mantra." I LOVE it. Ashley Wallen, the choreographer of the commercial, would down the road become the main choreographer of *Showman*.

You see how these things come together when you follow your joy? Hugh had a strong internal pull toward doing The Boy from Oz on Broadway, even though many people told him it wasn't a wise career move. In addition to the other doors it opened up, it led to him being asked to host the Oscars. His "I'll give it a go" response to that invitation led to the producer suggesting the Barnum musical, and to the commercial shoot where he met Michael Gracey, who would become his co-visionary on the project.

Continuing his hop around the world, Hugh took a quick trip to Shanghai to film his cameo role in *Snow Flower and the Secret Fan*. His friend Wendi Murdoch was producing so she had asked if he would play the nightclub owner. That scene reportedly was Jun Ji-hyun's first on-screen kiss – not a bad place to start! Hugh essentially played himself – a charming, successful Australian who loves to sing. Well, other than his character's callous womanizer thing. And no surprise, he had a blast. "I did pinch myself a little bit, coming here [to Shanghai], singing [with a 20-piece big band], bit of dancing, you know. It's been fun." Although he said it took him two months to phonetically learn the song he sang in Chinese.

Several movie roles Hugh was interested in were stalling in development. He loved the script of *Prisoners* which had originally been scheduled to film in 2009 but was delayed. *Avon Man* had been scheduled to start shooting that spring with Hugh both as a producer and in the title role, but was delayed.

In the movie business, or in any entrepreneurial endeavor really, we can find power in realizing that when one door closes, others will open. If we spend too much time worrying about things that aren't falling into place, we might miss other opportunities that are popping up! If something isn't going smoothly, it's ok to take a few deep breaths and realize it might not be the right time for that yet, and to look around for what's next!

Hugh jokes about always being on the lookout for a script that requires him to fatten up, and he found it in *Selma.* He put on 30 pounds preparing to play the sheriff in that film which had been scheduled to start shooting in May, but then that project fell through when the director switched to another film. It turned out that had him nice and plump for the role of Boyd Bolton in *Butter,* Jennifer Garner's first adventure as a producer. It only took one week to film his part, but he said it was "so much fun!"

It's amusing to note that Hugh told Martha Stewart his most embarrassing moment on a movie set happened while filming *Butter.* Because his love scene with Jennifer Garner is only heard, not seen, they had to perform just the audio. They recorded in the back seat of a car for authenticity, but the sound guy couldn't capture both their performances at once, so they had to create the sound one at a time. Hugh said he was really glad Jennifer went first because she took things way farther than he would have. Then when it was his turn, she was laughing so hard she was pressing her face into the seat in front of her to stifle the sound!

Once school was out, the family went off to Detroit for the filming of *Real Steel.* Hugh's boxing coach for the role was none other than Sugar Ray Leonard. Hugh said, "I was a little intimidated meeting him at first, particularly getting in the ring and sort of boxing with him." Leonard was impressed with Hugh. "He's a good student. He listens well. He takes it in and digests what I say, and it comes to life."

That project is another example of how delightful it is to watch Hugh work with child actors. Dakota Goyo's dad says Hugh "made my son feel like he was on top of the world!" One of my favorite lines of the movie, "Are you kidding me with those eyes?" wasn't in the script – it was an in-the-moment ad lib!

That fall Hugh officially stepped away from the *Avon Man* project because things seemed to be falling into place to film the second Wolverine movie with Darren Aronofsky directing. He started the intense workouts and eating to bulk up. They decided to close down their production company and focus on the things they really loved to do. *Smart.* Deb got her turn on Sesame Street for National Adoption Awareness Week, talking about forever families with Elmo. And an adorable French bulldog puppy (who would eventually come to be known as Dali) joined the family.

Oprah was on her Ultimate Australian Adventure and asked Hugh to be part of the grand finale in Sydney that December. Unbeknownst to Deb, their trip down under would also include one of the few times in their marriage Hugh kept a secret from her. She was surprised with an episode of *This Is Your Life* honoring her career, with family and friends from around the world in attendance or sending video messages.

But the Oprah taping brought a surprise of its own. The plan was for Hugh to make a dramatic entrance on a zipline from the roof of the opera house, but it got a little more dramatic than intended when the brake didn't work and Hugh crashed into the rigging above the stage. He tried to remain calm, mostly because his kids were in the audience, and asked for a tissue, but a tad more than that was needed!

After being stitched up by paramedics and medicated with a glass of red wine, Hugh went on with the show, including introducing Oprah to Vegemite. And then another of my favorite Hugh musical moments – singing "I Still Call Australia Home" with a huge choir, instrumental musicians, and a hometown crowd of 6,000 of his biggest fans. Hugh sang the first verse then was joined by none other than his childhood crush, Olivia Newton-John. Knowing how starstruck Hugh was meeting her ten years previously, I can only imagine how he felt singing a duet with her. Keith Urban, Nicole Kidman, and Russell Crowe all join in for the final verse.

Thankfully, the holidays provided some rest and healing time.

Early in 2011, Hugh did a few reshoots for *Real Steel*, including the scene where he comes to tell Max they got the Zeus fight. The visual effects team had to digitally "shrink" his neck and shoulders since he was much more bulked up than he had been the previous summer. Because of the reshoots, Hugh looked a lot like Charlie Kenton while doing advance press for the movie at the Super Bowl along with Sugar Ray. Another boyhood dream was coming true as he stood on the sideline talking to the press before the game started. That was early February and Hugh said in an interview that he was "about to do" Wolverine. And when he presented at the Oscars at the end of that month he said they would start shooting in Japan in the next couple months.

In March it became public knowledge that Aronofsky had backed out of directing Wolverine 2, so the film was delayed once again, and Hugh's schedule for the year was up in the air. He couldn't commit to another project with this big one hanging in limbo. How did Hugh handle it? It seems like the conventional wisdom in that situation would say he had two choices: to either "be patient and wait" or to "dig in and make it happen." *But in true Joy Revolution fashion, he chose a third option*, and used the delay as an excuse to try something that had been simmering in his head for a while that would be a more flexible time commitment: putting together a one-man musical show of his favorite songs! *#whatwouldHughdo*

Hugh enlisted Patrick Vaccariello, the musical director of *The Boy from Oz,* to help him put it all together and conduct the orchestra. He fit in a few little adventures in the meantime, like running the New York City half marathon to raise money for Shoe4africa, attending the FICCI-Frames film convention in India, and – drumroll please – he joined the world of social media. Hugh tweeted for the first time on April 24, 2011.

The Curran Theatre in San Francisco jumped at the chance to host Hugh's debut one-man show that May. It was a bit of an experiment, but was very well received, and Hugh saw the future potential. In a radio interview he said he'd love to do some version of the show periodically for the rest of his life. (I'm in for that.)

And something else exciting was taking shape, too. After Tom Hooper won an Oscar for directing *The King's Speech,* a rumor started circulating that his next project would be a movie version of the musical *Les Miserables.* A movie musical was still on Hugh's mental dream board, and the P.T. Barnum story was still a long shot, so why not go for one of the greatest musicals ever written? Cameron Mackintosh was producing (who had also produced *Oklahoma!* in London) and he wanted Hugh to play Javert. But Hugh was salivating over the part of Jean Valjean, which he considers the "holy grail" of acting roles. Cameron was unconvinced since Hugh doesn't naturally have a high tenor range, so Hugh asked if he could audition.

That audition happened in June, and well, it was memorable in many ways. (If you want to hear Hugh tell you about it himself—hilarious and definitely worth your time—Google his SAG-AFTRA Career Conversation with Jenelle Riley.) He had planned to warm up with his voice teacher then take a quick bike ride through the streets of Manhattan to the audition. Arriving at the teacher's studio, he noticed someone on the steps eyeing his bike, so he wrapped the lock several times around the frame. When he came out, the frame was there but the wheels were gone! (He now understands that's not uncommon. You have to thread your lock through the wheels, too.) A quick mental examination of his options—he couldn't fit the frame into a cab—left him all-out running 20 blocks with his bike frame on his shoulder, then up three flights of stairs to arrive sweaty and exhausted to the audition for his dream role. They kindly told him to sit down and catch his breath.

Hugh said it's the only audition he has ever asked to leave. He realized he'd been there almost three hours, and he needed to get home to put the kids to bed (Deb was out of town). From Hooper's perspective, that audition was pivotal in his decision to go ahead with the movie. "Hugh showed me the film was possible." Hugh was not only comfortable expressing himself through song, the physical act of singing made the emotion even deeper than acting through spoken dialogue. Tom didn't let Hugh know all that on that day, though. He made him wait a couple weeks before he called and told him the part was his.

He enjoyed a couple other performances that month also, with slightly lower stakes. On June 8 he performed again with Richard Marx at a concert in Chicago. (This time he nailed all the lyrics.) His rendition of To Where You Are is on the list of my requests for my funeral. It's heart-melting. A few days later he joined Neil Patrick Harris for a duet at the Tony Awards. For most people, singing at the Tonys wouldn't be a "low stakes" event, but that's Hugh's idea of a fun night out!

Another milestone... Hugh posted on Facebook for the first time on June 17. He said he went onto social media begrudgingly, mostly because there were so many accounts pretending to be him, he wanted to slow that down by having a real presence. (There are still plenty of fake celebrity accounts unfortunately, trying to convince unsuspecting social media novices to "donate" to one cause or another. Those donations of course end up in the swindler's pocket.) He's had love/hate moments with the different platforms, but now he has fun with it. An unexpected side benefit is it has cut down somewhat on the paparazzi! There's not as much value in a photograph of Hugh coming out of the gym if he just posted a selfie during his workout!

In July, Hugh took his one-man show to Toronto. The family went along of course, as they usually do, especially during summer vacation. Oscar surprised Hugh by asking if he could be in the show on opening night, playing didgeridoo during Over the Rainbow. (I have purposely not included many stories about Oscar and Ava, so that they can tell their own story in their own timing if they wish. But that one is too sweet to leave out.)

After a quick trip to Comic-Con doing more advance promotion for *Real Steel,* the family took off for a vacation in France. (Hugh jokingly called it research for *Les Mis.*) Toward the end of that trip he filmed another Lipton commercial in Budapest.

I can't help but note that instead of pounding the pavement trying to wrangle the pieces into place for Wolverine 2, Hugh's decision to *let that timing work itself out and focus on other things he loves* was paying off. His one-man show was receiving enthusiastic acclaim, and other musical projects were moving forward. **In August of 2011, Michael Gracey was officially announced as the director of the P.T. Barnum musical in development.** In September, Hugh's casting as Jean Valjean was made official, and he announced that his one man show would come to Broadway for ten weeks! In an interview on the Jonathan Ross show, Hugh said he would love to bring the one-man show to the UK. Finally in 2019 that dream came true!

It could have been a frustrating year, but during the promotional appearances for *Real Steel,* there's no doubt Hugh was enjoying life. The world premiere was on September 6 in Paris. This was the first live action movie of Hugh's that the kids had seen, and part way through watching it, Hugh and Deb both realized it would be the first time the kids would see Hugh kiss another woman on screen. I'm sure that bit was way overshadowed by the kids falling in love with Atom, the robot. No, wait. Ava's favorite robot was Noisy Boy.

After Paris they went on to red carpets in Moscow, London, Sydney, and Los Angeles. (The Japanese premiere was on November 29, but by then Hugh was performing on Broadway and couldn't attend.) And of course there were tons of interviews and appearances in between. On the Jonathan Ross show, he made his entrance being shot out of a cannon (well, ok, that part was actually a dummy). A Russian talk show orchestrated a flash mob of his dance from the Lipton commercials. He recreated his secondary school *Music Man* audition for Jay Leno. He broke a guy's jaw guest-starring on *WWE Monday Night Raw.* He reunited with his *In Fashion* co-stars on *Rove LA.* He even made a surprise cameo appearance on *Saturday Night Live,* impersonating Daniel Radcliffe (a slightly taller version). And he got soaked playing water war with Jimmy

Fallon. Not all actors love the publicity part of the business, but Hugh is a natural, always game for anything!

Once again, Hugh's schedule astounds me. After that whirlwind September, he spent October launching a coffee business, doing some early rehearsals for *Les Mis* in England (where he met the Queen), then doing final rehearsals for his one-man show on Broadway. Only someone who absolutely loves what they do could thrive at that pace.

Laughing Man Coffee co-founder David Steingard had become friends with Hugh through the School of Practical Philosophy. David's father had previously been in the coffee business, and had been starting to talk about going back into that business right at the time Hugh and Deb had come back from Ethiopia and were looking for a way to further support Dukale and his community. So Hugh suggested they collaborate, and Hugh would donate his share of the profits to charity.

Hugh and Deb have been very generous about donating both their resources and their voices to various causes. So why did Hugh want to start a company? He told the *Wall Street Journal*,

> *My capital is mainly my profile and how to use that. And so you can use that capital, for example, to bring awareness to an organization—you become an ambassador. And the moment your capital is gone—your career's gone or you die—that's sort of over. Or you can be someone like Paul Newman, who uses the capital to actually create something, which creates jobs, that actually creates a great product that benefits people. And sadly, Paul Newman's no longer here, and yet his organization is giving hundreds of millions of dollars away, plus 1,000 or 1,500 jobs a year. And I thought that is the smartest way to use capital.*

With a career like Hugh's it's hard to imagine a context in which he would need to "think bigger," but that's exactly what he was doing with Laughing Man. Yes, he and Deb have an above-average capacity to donate to causes, and to bring awareness to issues as spokespeople, but they both have gone beyond that—creating organizations that take on a life of their own. What are your wild and crazy dreams for your legacy?

Laughing Man officially launched on October 12, 2011, Hugh's 43rd birthday. The name of the company was inspired by the title of a J.D. Salinger short story (the content of the story has no connection to the business, they just liked the name). They liked the image those words portrayed of a moment of laughter that makes "all differences fade away." (Steingard's words.) The motto, All Be Happy, comes from a sanskrit prayer:

> *May all be happy*
> *May all be free of disease*
> *May all have well-being*
> *And none suffer misery of any kind*
> *May peace be everywhere*

They started with the 150 sq. ft café in Tribeca, buying coffee straight from Dukale's co-op. At the kick-off event, Hugh paid tribute to Dukale as their inspiration: "Never in a million years could I have envisioned that today I would be – it gives me chills – I would be launching, in his honor, a coffee named after him." The coffee is delicious, and growth happened organically. When the Oculus transportation hub was being built in Manhattan, the developers approached Laughing Man to open a second location there, because their CEO had stopped into the Duane St café and had a great experience.

Start small and do what you do really well. That's a pretty good business plan.

Hugh appeared on Martha Stewart to promote *Real Steel,* Laughing Man, and his Broadway show. Lots going on! They made banana bread, and Hugh proved he's pretty handy in the kitchen. "Should I do some washing up while you finish?" he asked Martha.

And then Hugh was on back on Broadway again, setting more box office records! "I'm not exaggerating. He is the top Broadway draw now," Albert Poland (general manager of *The Boy From Oz*) told the *New York Post*. "Hugh generates the same kind of excitement as a Judy Garland. He's the only person I would ever compare to her."

It's notable that it was the first time Deb wasn't able to be there for one of Hugh's opening nights on stage. National Adoption Awareness Week was taking shape in Australia, so she was on the other side of the world participating in that milestone of her "advocist" work. Isn't that a great word? I think Deb made it up accidentally but I'm stealing it! A particularly memorable show was the one on October 27, the same night as the suspenseful game six of the World Series between the Cardinals and the Rangers. Hugh could tell there were many baseball fans whose minds were elsewhere that night so he did his best to keep them updated on the score from the stage. Near the end of the show he hadn't checked in a while so asked the audience if anyone knew the score, and dozens of people shouted it out! But at most performances there were no such distractions. The *New York Times* called Hugh a "master of mass flirtation."

Hugh continued his own charitable work with an auction after every show to raise money for Broadway Cares Equity Fights Aids, just as he had done with *A Steady Rain*. At the Gypsy of the Year fundraiser, Hugh was given special recognition for already having raised over $800,000 in the first three weeks of his show! His wry sense of humor was alive and well. "You have no idea how much sex I've been having, it's unbelievable," he said, explaining his success. Just kidding, all he was doing was selling his sweaty undershirts for up to $25,000 each night. (!!) By the end of the run, the show raised almost $1.8 million for the cause.

He probably couldn't have auctioned his clothes for that much if he had stuck with journalism. That's the power of finding what you were born to do!

By then a firm plan had finally come together for shooting the second Wolverine movie the following summer, so Hugh was able to announce in his TV appearances that winter that it was coming! (Whoopi Goldberg especially wanted to know the latest when he was on *The View*.) By staying positive and doing something else fun when things were stalled, the door opened up for Hugh to work again with *Kate & Leopold* director James Mangold, which would provide his most satisfying Wolverine experience yet. Oh, and one more important milestone: in December Hugh's twitter account reached one million followers.

In January of 2012 Hugh picked up another People's Choice Award for Favorite Action Movie Star for *Real Steel*. The following year would prove to be even more eventful on the awards front...

CHAPTER 8

OSCAR'S DAD EARNS AN OSCAR NOMINATION

It was the "holy grail" of acting roles indeed. Or the Mt. Everest. In February of 2012, Hugh left for England to begin rehearsals for his first movie musical, *Les Miserables*. It was the second time he made a feature film without his family traveling along, partly because the kids were in school, and partly because he knew it would be emotionally and physically exhausting, even more than *The Fountain* had been. They kept to their two week rule, though, either with Hugh flying home on weekends or Deb and the kids visiting him.

During their many weeks of rehearsal, Hugh and Russell Crowe (Jacko and Rusty, that is) teamed up to present Best Film at the BAFTA awards. Those two long-time friends are such a hoot together! Though they had been mates for a long time, *Les Mis* was their first opportunity to act together. So while the rehearsals were pretty intense, you also get a sense of how closely bonded the cast was.

Intense really is an understatement. The combination of what Hugh was doing to prepare his physique for the film (he lost 30 pounds while keeping sharp muscle definition), the emotional intensity of the character, and the vocal demands of singing an incredibly difficult part live take after take, are more than I can imagine one person being able to do. In fact, at one point, while they were rehearsing Valjean's death scene, Hugh started thinking it was more than what was humanly possible for him. It was about three weeks before they were to start shooting. He'd been really frustrated with himself that day and felt others were frustrated with him, too. Thankfully Deb was visiting. He told her at the end of the day, "Babe, I may have bitten off more than I can chew here. I know I always wanted to play this part but it's so massive, and every scene is so massive, I don't know. I'm wondering if I should just sort of own up and say this is the time to walk out, that someone else should play this part."

Deb was unequivocal. She said that's exactly how a person would feel playing Jean Valjean if they're really grasping that character, but that Hugh was going to "nail it."

And somehow, Deb's confidence in him gave him superhuman abilities.

I have to point out that I have great respect for someone who walks away when they really don't think they're able to complete something, for whatever reason. If it's possible someone else could step in and do it better, then it's gracious to not let pride stop you from handing it over. And in most cases it's not worth killing yourself trying to do what's beyond you. But I also know that Deb's belief in Hugh was genuine. If she had agreed that it wasn't going to work, she would have fully supported his backing out. But she saw his potential, better than he saw it himself, and – equally important – he believed her when she said it.

I also don't think there's another actor alive who could have done better. The sum of the physical, emotional, and vocal ability that role required was insane. Tom Hooper agreed. "I personally would not have made the film if Hugh Jackman did not exist." Tom explained that in addition to his abilities, Hugh "carries in him an extraordinary kindness and compassion" which enabled him to portray the spiritual depth of the character. The only thing I wish is that Hugh would have insisted on taking some of those arias back down to the original octave, which would have better matched the groundedness he embodied in Jean Valjean. (And I selfishly always want to hear more of Hugh's rich lower range.) The actors all agreed that when singing live, in pursuit of a visceral level of realness not seen in a musical before, it was less important for the singing to be "pretty" than for the raw emotion to be felt by the audience.

Did I mention filming was intense? Tom Hooper again: "Hugh was up to his chest in freezing cold sea water, he was up a mountain singing and wearing bare feet and wooden clogs in minus 5 degrees, he was singing and [weight] training every day, and he was always gracious." And that was even while giving up coffee for the duration of the project for maximum hydration! They shot for 14 weeks, and the physical transformation during that time was remarkable. For most of the rehearsal period, Hugh was doing heavy workouts while eating extremely low carb in order to bulk up but still have a gauntness befitting a prisoner. The final effect was achieved by Hugh going without water for 36 hours to have that sunken, emaciated look, resulting in a terrible headache and tightness in his chest. It's really something to put your body through that for the sake of your art. Hugh's beard was getting pretty long, but they still had to add extensions to it to achieve the look of prisoner Jean Valjean.

During filming, the cast tried not to talk too much when the cameras were off, to rest their voices. Hugh did a lot of jigsaw puzzles. Once the convict scenes were complete, at the end of March, Hugh shaved his beard, then had to rapidly fatten up to play the prosperous mayor. That transformation was more fun! Truly, though, Hugh didn't "fatten" up, as he had to be in Wolverine shape only a few weeks after finishing *Les Mis.* In fact, he wanted to be in more badass shape than ever for *The Wolverine,* so he sought advice from Dwayne (The Rock) Johnson, who recommended three hours a day in the gym and 6000 calories a day of chicken and steak.

At the 2012 Tony Awards on June 10, Deborra-lee repaid Hugh for his covert *This is Your Life* operation by pulling off the first time she's ever kept a secret from him, when she surprised him as the presenter of his Special Tony Award. She told him she was going to the bathroom, so he was perturbed when she wasn't back in time, thinking she was going to miss his moment. His look of wonder when they announced her as the next presenter was priceless. He added as he accepted the award, "I know how much you hate public speaking! This is probably the greatest thing you've ever done for me." Filming was almost complete on *Les Mis*, and while they had squeezed in short visits every two weeks, those months marked the most time apart they experienced in their marriage. He had flown home the night before the awards and was flying out again the next morning for four more days of filming.

A reporter asked that night whether *Houdini* was still in the works and he said yes, that they were doing a read through of the first act when he got back from London.

Hugh and Deb and the kids had a little recovery and reconnection time in Bali, then they went on to Sydney to prepare for the next big film!

It was Hugh's sixth time portraying Wolverine (counting the *First Class* cameo), but it was also a whole new world. There was a new cast surrounding him, a new director, a new setting, and new challenges. The whole family moved to Sydney, and the kids enrolled in school in Australia. They all went to Japan together for the portion filmed there, too, giving Hugh and Oscar the opportunity to climb Mt. Fuji together on a weekend in August.

Lauren Shuler Donner, who was a producer on all the X-Men movies, said it was the best Hugh had ever been as the character. Hugh credits the direction of James Mangold. "He really got the most out of all of us." I think the crew got the most out of the locations they used as well! The Chinese Gardens in Sydney were transformed into the set where Yashida's funeral was held. The whole ceremonial temple was built on pontoons so as not to disturb the wildlife living in the lake! And in a small town outside Sydney, they filmed at night using snow machines while it was 36 degrees (Celsius, or 97 degrees Fahrenheit)!

James' and Hugh's overriding intention was to tell a story that was true to the character without worrying about the film's rating, and in fact the final rating decision wasn't made until near the end of editing. Hugh's position was that character would come first, but if it ended up being R-rated, there had to be a really good reason he could explain to the teenage Wolverine fans who would stop him on the street.

Hugh loved being back in Australia again. While they were filming in a studio in Sydney, the Korean pop star PSY was on the adjoining soundstage filming an appearance on *X-Factor*. He popped over to the *Wolverine* set, put on a set of claws, and taught Hugh to dance Gangnam style! And since they were in the country, Hugh and Deb got to attend the Red Ball and the World Vision Ball, and headline National Adoption Awareness Week activities in November. Several of their friends in the Australian press did on-set interviews, and Hugh is at his most relaxed with home-town reporters, which is so fun to see. The best part, he said, was being able to swim at Bondi Beach every morning while shooting.

Just as *The Wolverine* filming wrapped, the animated feature *Rise of the Guardians* was released, in which we learn that the Easter Bunny (voiced by Hugh) is a somewhat curmudgeonly Australian with a slight resemblance to a kangaroo. Hugh celebrated completing the three-year process of getting *The Wolverine* made with a day of golf. But he had to be content with a very brief break, then went straight into promoting *Les Miserables*, starting in South Korea three days later.

Hugh said about seeing *Les Mis* for the first time, "I've never been more nervous to watch something." And according to Deb, that wasn't an exaggeration. She leaned over to him about an hour into the film and said, "I love your holding my hand but it's hurting." She said it wasn't easy for her to watch either, because it's hard to see him looking so emaciated and miserable. And how did he feel about the Oscar buzz? "I'm happy with what I did, so if any of that stuff comes up, great. And if it doesn't, I don't want to feel in any way like the movie is not good. I'm really proud of it."

That's such a healthy perspective. Recognition from others is nice, but the barometer that matters most is how you feel about your own work.

Dream of being in a movie musical: check! In an interview he mentioned that next he'd like to do a remake of *Guys and Dolls* or *Carousel*. *There are always new dreams popping up, because that's how we're designed! Your sweet spot is celebrating what you've done AND having a vision for what's next!*

After South Korea they headed home to New York, fitting in a quick trip to the London premiere on December 5. On December 8, Hugh and Deb attended a performance of Russell Crowe's band at Joe's Pub in Manhattan. Of course Rusty pulled Hugh up on stage for a couple of tunes: "The Letter" that he had done that summer with Richard Marx, and a reprise of "Confrontation" from *Les Mis. Even when life is busy, you have to fit in the fun!* The New York premiere was held on Monday, December 10. It kicked off quite a week.

That Wednesday Hugh was the subject of the Museum of Moving Images Salute in New York and learned he'd been nominated for a SAG award. Then Thursday, December 13, after taking a red-eye flight to Los Angeles and arriving in the wee hours of the morning, they slept a little bit then woke up to learn he was nominated for a Golden Globe. They got a few more hours of blissful sleep after that, then headed for the ceremony unveiling the Hugh Jackman star on the Hollywood Walk of Fame. Hugh was nominated for this recognition by his long-time fan page, Jackman's Landing, founded in 2000 by Pat Bates. I loved his joke about getting the star in place before the end of the Mayan calendar! The day continued with teaching (or trying to teach) Jay Leno some Gangnam Style moves, and paying Ellen DeGeneres a visit. I think it was on the same trip – the next day I hope – that he filmed his second appearance on *Inside the Actors Studio* with James Lipton. Whew!

Their travel continued with premieres in Japan and Australia. By then his beard for *Prisoners* was starting to become evident, and the upcoming project *X-Men: Days of Future Past* was announced! Then – exhale slowly – quiet holidays in New York. Well, likely with a lot of time spent researching and preparing for the next role coming up quickly.

Shooting for *Prisoners* began in Georgia in January. And while driving to the set on Thursday, January 10, 2013, Hugh learned he was nominated for an Academy Award. Thus began a few months of sharp contrast. Hugh remarked on the strangeness of filming a very emotionally intense story during the week and attending glitzy events every weekend. It started that very night with the Critics' Choice Awards, the AFI Awards the next night, the G'Day USA gala on Saturday evening, then the Golden Globes Sunday night, where Hugh won! The tears in Deb's eyes as she kissed him when his name was called melt my heart. But the celebration had to be minimal, as not only was Hugh still recovering from a respiratory flu, he had to be back on set in Georgia the following morning.

Two weeks later they were back in Los Angeles for the SAG Awards. I think the funniest moment of the night was when Hugh and Anne introduced *Les Mis* this way: "Wolverine is being chased by Gladiator. Catwoman gets knocked up and for some ungodly reason goes to see Bellatrix Lestrange and Borat. Then Wolverine agrees to raise Catwoman's baby, who grows up to star in Mamma Mia."

Another week of filming, then back to Los Angeles for the Oscars luncheon, the Directors Guild of America Awards, and another appearance on *The Tonight Show*. Hugh said he felt short on sleep for much of the time filming *Prisoners*, but it fit his character so he used it! The director, Denis Villeneuve, said the movie was a joy to make because he felt that everyone "was doing it for the love of cinema, not for ambition, but an act of creation." *For the love of it. The strongest motivation.* Denis also recalled that Hugh was constantly eating on set – it seemed like every time he turned around Hugh had a plate of chicken. Of course Hugh was bulking back up for the next X-Men production.

That film is heavy and dark. Here's how Jake Gyllenhaal described one of the pivotal scenes they had together.

> *There's a scene where I'm showing Hugh the pictures of the bloody children's clothes. And the scene was written as Keller throwing me up against the wall and strangling me and saying, 'This is your fault! You did this!' in a really violent way. And on the day of that scene – and we really didn't have a lot of time – I remember Hugh coming up and saying, 'I just don't feel right about doing this. He's going to be so physical with Paul's character, I really think it's much more cutting if he just sat there and said to him 'This is your fault. You wasted time.' What ensued was Denis saying 'I love that idea.' And in my opinion, that's some of the best*

acting I've ever witnessed in front of me, and some of the most vulnerable acting I've ever seen from an actor.

Back to the awards glamor, they were off to Europe for the Berlinale Film Festival Saturday night and the BAFTAs Sunday night. A reporter asked Hugh on the red carpet if it was even worth showing up when Daniel Day-Lewis is nominated in the same category. It takes a special person to give a gracious answer to that one, which of course Hugh did. In fact, Hugh showed his sense of humor by showing up on David Letterman wearing a stovepipe hat and Lincoln-esque beard, to "sway a few last minute Oscar voters."

The Academy Awards were on Sunday night, February 24. There aren't enough superlatives in my vocabulary to describe the cast's performance of One Day More. No matter how many times I watch the video, when Hugh steps out and starts with the opening of "Suddenly," my goosebumps start, and they only grow as each cast member joins him. Anne Hathaway's acceptance speech for Supporting Actress in which she thanked Hugh for his amazing support was heartwarming, and in her backstage interview she referred to him as a "magical alien combination of strength and soul and heart and artistry and fun." And I think an equally sweet moment of the evening was when Jennifer Lawrence fell on the stairs going up to accept her award, and Hugh was out of his chair moving to help her so quickly it was astonishing.

The contrast continued as he went back to Atlanta to the far less glossy world of two families' trauma and terror. Hugh said he certainly hugged his kids a little tighter while filming that story.

Meanwhile, what was going on with the P.T. Barnum musical? The original plan for the music was for a lot of different popular songwriters to write one song each that would make up the soundtrack. So a lot of composers wrote sample songs. But the one that stood out the most wasn't from a big name. Justin Paul and Benj Pasek were at that point a very young, barely known musical theater duo. They were in California working on writing *Dear Evan Hansen*, when a colleague of Michael Gracey's suggested they meet with him since they wrote music. Justin described it to *Deadline*:

Within a matter of days, we found ourselves in a room with Michael, who had no idea who we were, and had no reason to. But he, like a champ, pitched the film, what his vision of it was going to be. He pitched it as this timeless tale of P.T. Barnum inventing the American circus, and really leaned into the fact that it was a man who was ahead of his time.

He wanted the music to be contemporary. We thought that was really bizarre and intriguing, and that was one of the reasons that we really perked up. It was this period tale, but he said, 'The choreography is going to be contemporary, the music wants to be contemporary.'

They wrote "A Million Dreams" and it knocked Michael's socks off. They began working in collaboration to nail down the sound that matched Michael's vision. The next hurdle was convincing the studio execs to consider these youngsters in the mix with the best-known songwriters in the world. There may have been a few little "exaggerations" of their credentials involved in that approval, such as a made up Tony award... For the next couple years there were still a variety of composers who wrote songs that were tried in workshops before it became crystal clear that the entire soundtrack would be done by Pasek and Paul.

Michael Gracey's vision was so clear and so strong, it stuck in other people's heads, too—even colleagues of colleagues—and that created the path to connect him with the perfect collaborators. Those songs are permeating our thoughts in a way that has begun to change our culture.

Hugh and Deb celebrated their 17th wedding anniversary at home in New York, then they were off to Montreal for the filming of *X-Men: Days of Future Past!* Hugh remembers exactly when the nude scene was filmed – May 21, 2013. In each Wolverine movie he planned his workout and nutrition schedule carefully around when key scenes were to be filmed so he could be in peak condition. At one point the director said they might move the date for shooting that scene. Hugh's response was something like, "You can film whichever scene you want, but that's the day I'm taking my clothes off." He said he always did a few pushups moments before the camera rolled for maximum effect of veins popping out, etc. And "particularly for the butt shot, a few extra lunges." Good work, Hugh. Very effective. As he stood looking in the mirror while they got focus marks, he thought, "I'm never going to look like this again." (Meanwhile back at home, Madame Tussaud's unveiled a wax figure of Hugh as Wolverine. With clothes.)

A week later Oprah interviewed Hugh. They discussed a lot of deep topics, but the funniest moment was when she put her arm around him at the end for a photo and then couldn't stop gushing about the ab definition she could feel! Hugh never had help from CGI or steroids in achieving his Wolverine look, but he did admit to a "fair bit" of fake tan. So what were his secrets? Most important, as he told Oprah that day, is that he truly enjoys working out! "I'm someone who likes routine and discipline. I kind of revel when I've got a structure." And it seems he loved going farther and farther with the character in each film.

The combination, though, of waking up at 3:30 am to work out, then spending a lot of time on set lying on his back on a concrete slab with his eyes closed, meant it was common for him to fall asleep during takes! Since Ellen Page's role was to sit at his head with her hands on either side of his face, she did a lot of tapping his cheek to wake him up. But of course there was plenty of action as well – flying backward through the air on ropes during the stadium scene, for example. They shot the portion with the old cast first, I mean – ahem – the original cast, then the younger, with one day of overlap for Patrick Stewart and James McAvoy's scene together.

While they continued filming without him, Hugh left to promote *The Wolverine.* Usually when Hugh is doing press for a movie, his look is completely different from what he's promoting, having moved on to some other character. But in this case, since he made X-Men movies two years in a row, he looked like Wolverine at all those appearances, which added an extra level of buzz to every audience.

They started in South Korea on July 15, where Hugh showed off his Gangnam Style moves with the Korean pop group Sistar. There were massive screaming crowds in London at the July 16 premiere with lots of press the next day, including an appearance on *Top Gear,* which produced my all-time favorite GIF of Hugh laughing. At Comic-Con he promoted both *The Wolverine* and *Days of Future Past,* then zipped back to New York. David Letterman asked him if it was a lot of work to be in Wolverine condition. "No, I was pretty much born this way," Hugh dead-panned. Then he was on Jimmy Fallon's first show since Jimmy became a father. "I'm your first interview with no sleep!" Hugh exclaimed. They had a hilarious conversation about "babyproofing Wolverine" with rubber-coated "clamps." (Yes, Jimmy's sleep-deprivation was showing when he couldn't think of the word "claws.") They played a game of, uh, beer bean bag, I suppose you would call it.

In another social media milestone, Hugh posted on Instagram for the first time on July 31, 2013. Predicting a future pattern, it was a photo of their dog, Dali.

While wrapping up filming in Montreal, Hugh had his turn to be the primary parent while Deb traveled to Africa with the Clinton Global Initiative. The delegation studied adoption policy and the situation of orphans in six different countries. It's so amazing to watch Deb's journey toward being one of the world's top advocates for kids who need permanent families. She wasn't looking for a cause, wasn't looking to be a leader, she just spoke out when she saw injustice and it grew from there.

After that trip, she wrote a guest editorial for CNN.com about the state of children in the world. This paragraph beautifully sums up her passion:

> *I am not a learned scholar or professional worker in international adoption. I am not even an adoption advocate -- I am a **child** advocate. I am an individual who has witnessed what life is like for children who don't have anyone to watch their back, or teach them right from wrong, to care about what they think or feel, or the basic human need to feel loved, to feel safe and secure and to feel that they actually matter. I believe everyone deserves be the object of someone's affection.*

I love this so much because while it's bringing attention to the situation of children who don't have a family, it creates a mental picture of what we DO want—the description of why family and belonging matter. That's why she's so solution-focused. The picture in her autopilot brain is of all children having a loving family.

Hugh was excited to bring *The Wolverine* to Japan for the premiere there at the end of August. He went straight from the plane to a talk show appearance, waiting to sleep until afterward. Practice traveling around the world evidently makes it easier! By then his mutton chops were gone, indicating that the filming of *Days of Future Past* was complete. It was the end of two and a half years straight of Hugh being on his Wolverine nutrition and workout regimen. For the "first time in 14 years," there was nothing coming up that Hugh had to be in shape for. So he told Deb he was going to do whatever he wanted for a few months. After three or four DAYS of not going to the gym, he missed it so started going again! But he did enjoy eating whatever food he wanted.

A makeup artist on set had mentioned what seemed to be a recurring sore on his nose, but Hugh assumed he had poked himself with the claws. He didn't take time then to see a doctor about it, possibly because he went right into promoting *Prisoners*, which premiered at the Toronto International Film Festival (TIFF) in early September.

At the TIFF press conference there was a lot of Oscar talk. Hugh's co-stars fed it. Jake Gyllenhaal said, "If you're asking me if I think that Hugh Jackman deserves an Oscar, the answer to that question is absolutely yes." (The question hadn't originally been directed at him, but I'm happy he jumped in.) Terrence Howard concurred, that even though he's plenty tall and strong himself, and he knows Hugh is a sweet man, being right next to him in some of the most intense scenes was physically frightening. Maria Bello commented that her only regret was playing Hugh's wife and never getting a chance to touch his lips or feel his abs. ☺ She then added that it was Hugh's "strength of just going for it and never faltering – that's what makes the movie work." Perhaps the best compliment to Hugh's acting was Deb's reaction to the character. Hugh recalled that while watching the movie for the first time, Deb was gripping his hand so hard her nails left marks. But as the story intensified, she removed her hand as it became uncomfortable to be connected with the person on the screen.

They had a week at home in New York (time to cheer on Serena Williams at the US Open, learn lawn bowling, and take in an NFL game) before the full-on press tour began. Katie Couric arranged a meeting of the Hugh Jackman/Jake Gyllenhaal Mutual Adoration Society on her show, which is both incredibly sweet and hilarious. But Hugh can trash talk like a pro, too, as evidenced in his arm wrestling match with Jimmy Fallon.

An unusual stop on that press tour was Iowa Falls, Iowa, Patrick Whitesell's hometown. Sadly, the timing didn't work out for Hugh and family to get to see the butter sculptures at the Iowa State Fair. Maybe someday. ☺ In any case, Patrick's father had restored the Metropolitan Theater in town, and in gratitude for Patrick's support of Hugh's career, the celebration of the venue's reopening included a double feature of *Prisoners* and *The Wolverine!* The whole family was along and got to do some fishing. Even Dali got to come on that trip and walk the red carpet! From there Hugh went on to London, Paris, Berlin, San Sebastian, and Zurich—you know, destinations comparable to Iowa. Hugh received the Donostia Award at the San Sebastian International Film Festival and the Golden Icon Award at the Zurich Film Festival.

In one of their joint interviews, Jake made the comment about Hugh, "Given his position, he can make any movie get made, really." Hugh kept a poker face, but I wonder if the P.T. Barnum musical popped into his mind. Since it didn't seem to be going anywhere, he would have been justified in thinking Jake was overstating his power. He was more optimistic at that point about bringing the original musical *Houdini* to life on Broadway.

Once publicity for *Prisoners* was finished, Hugh finally did take a break, focusing for the rest of the year on things like being the assistant coach of Oscar's soccer team. Which is good, because Deb's work was heating up!

Deborra-lee was awarded the first National Angel in Adoption Award from the Congressional Coalition on Adoption Institute on October 9 in Washington DC. Then Hugh celebrated his birthday by doing a One Night Only one-man show/fundraiser for the Motion Picture Television Fund! That night was a shining example of what the Joy Revolution is all about – how you can light up the world doing what you love. As he told *The Hollywood Reporter,* "A lot of guys would say to their wife, 'Do you mind if I go play golf with my buddies?' That's how I am about the show. I love it. If there's a song I don't like, I cut it and bring in a new song. Everything is something I want to do." And he raised almost $2 million in one night. Once again his sweaty undershirts – one from the first half of the show and another from the second half – sold for $11,000 each in his post-show auction. After a little celebrating, Hugh took off at midnight that night (as you do) on a flight to Beijing for the Chinese premiere of *The Wolverine.*

In November, Deb headed to Australia for National Adoption Awareness Week. Jules Allen, a foster and adoptive mother, spent the week with Deb and had this to say about the experience:

> *It was during this week I developed a deep and powerful respect for Deb, not only as an amazing dynamo of a woman, but as an incredibly authentic, motivated and driven inspirer for this cause. She was up at 4am each day, enthusiastic about the day ahead, bounding from one engagement to the next, treating every person who came into her sphere with the same respect as the last. Her warmth and compassion would permeate throughout every room she entered.*

Part of Deb's power to effect change is that she always believes solutions exist. That kind of focus is how you, too, can keep your energy up during frustrating times. And it keeps your brain always on the lookout for opportunities!

When she got back, Deb finally convinced Hugh to get the spot on his nose looked at, and he learned it was basal cell carcinoma. If you have to hear the word cancer, that's the "good" kind, and they removed the spot. And on that day, Hugh learned the best side of social media. Someone recognized him in the doctor's waiting room, and he figured that within about 17 minutes, exaggerated reports of his impending demise would be circulating on the internet. Instead, he snapped a selfie and posted the real details on Instagram.

A couple weeks later, Hugh and Deb were honored with the Lifetime of Giving Award at the David Lynch Foundation gala. Although the night was about the benefits of meditation, everyone had questions about cancer and the bandage on his nose. The next week Hugh filmed an episode as a guest judge on the reality TV show *Ink Master,* evaluating tattoos of X-Men characters, including two of himself. To round out the variety that is his life, he hosted *Christmas in Washington* with the Obama family.

Mid-December found them all in Australia, with Deb announcing the "birth" of Adopt Change, the non-profit organization that grew out of National Adoption Awareness Week. Its goal is to shift the Australian culture away from anti-adoption toward a holistic, ethical approach to the adoption process. I get so inspired listening to Deb talk about this issue, for which she has such passion. She gets right to the heart of the matter. She's not intimidated by a challenge, she just figures out where to start, then keeps going. She knew that systemic change would require a vocal champion within the government, so she kept at it until she found that person in Prime Minister Tony Abbott.

In a setting that would have intimidated a lot of people, stepping to the microphone right after the Prime Minister, Deb said, with a huge grin, "I just want to savor this moment." *She is full of Joy, and she brings her authentic self into every situation. She is my hero.*

Hugh must have been feeling like it was time to wipe the slate clean and stop putting energy into projects that were hitting roadblocks. Things had stalled with *Houdini,* so just before Christmas he called the producers and pulled himself out of it.

There is wisdom in knowing when to persist and when to shift your energy elsewhere. In Hugh's case, I wonder if it's because his schedule had slowed down enough that he had time to reflect and reassess – sort of a

121

strategic planning retreat for himself. When things aren't going smoothly, it's a good time to step back and take a breath. Here are some questions you can ask yourself, maybe writing in a journal.

- *Does my vision for the outcome still excite me?*
- *Are things moving in the right direction?*
- *Are other people I enjoy working with still excited about this?*
- *Am I excited about the specific reality of this, or just the general idea of it?*
- *Is this something I feel like I'm supposed to want, or do I really want it?*

So I applaud Hugh's decision. But I also keep thinking, somewhere on a shelf in someone's office, there's a collection of songs written with Hugh in mind by Stephen Schwartz, the composer of *Wicked*. I'd love to hear them!

What about the other original musical he'd been developing? It seemed like it was headed for the same fate. While in Australia for the holidays, Hugh asked Michael Gracey to come and meet with him about the future of the P.T. Barnum story. At that point Hugh and Michael had been working on the project for more than four years, and Hugh was starting to feel it would probably never happen. It didn't seem to be gaining the needed traction, so he didn't want Michael spending any more time and energy on it. They talked for about 45 minutes in Hugh and Deb's hotel suite, Hugh sharing his concerns and Michael countering with his vision for what it could be – a memorable, uplifting experience for all ages. By the end of that conversation, Hugh was back on board and more excited than ever. He joked, "I went into that room to break up, and came out pregnant."

Hugh unwittingly hit on one of the best analogies I've ever heard (from Abraham Hicks) for the power of vision to bring a dream to reality – pregnancy. At first the idea of getting pregnant is just that, an idea. Then there's a moment in time when the pieces come together and an embryo implants. A couple who is pregnant doesn't have a baby yet, but the joy and excitement they feel is very real. It's the same with a dream that "takes hold" inside you. It becomes part of who you are and grows as you feed it.

And here's a powerful part of the analogy: how does the pregnant woman make the baby grow? What action does she need to take every day? She only needs to take care of herself – nutrition, rest, hydration, etc. The body will naturally do what it needs to do. Did you know you can trust your brain with dreams the same way? When that vision is so clear that your autopilot brain is engaged, you can follow your instincts and take the action that gives you a thrill of excitement, and it will lead you toward your dream.

Here's the other powerful part – do dreams ever not work out in the way or the timing we're hoping for? Of course. Deb and Hugh can attest to that, along with all other couples who have experienced a pregnancy loss. Then what? They mourn. They allow themselves recovery time. Sometimes they seek more information. Sometimes they try other options. Rarely does the couple give up on the dream of becoming parents, because they innately know, and they see around them, that babies happen all the time. What if you could learn to be just as aware of all the dreams coming true around you, large and small, and that would help you see around life's curve balls to keep believing in your dreams?

This story also illustrates another key piece of the Joy Revolution. **We all need a Michael Gracey or two in our lives.** *We all have times when our Belief Engines slow down or start to pull backwards. Having someone who helps you refocus your vision is critical. I call that person a* **Focus Buddy**. *A lot of trainers use the term accountability partner, but I'm not a big fan of the word accountability. It's external. It's disempowering. Someone else holding a carrot or a stick will never be as powerful as the motivation that comes from being lit up inside. But we all need those friends and partners who can fan our flame when we lose focus and our belief wavers.*

Ok, back to our story.

Hugh checked off another boyhood dream by appearing on the Cricket Show on Boxing Day, then in January 2014 the family took off for Johannesburg, South Africa, for Hugh to film his part in *Chappie*. He'd been growing his hair out for a little over a month to prepare for that dazzling mullet. Since Hugh's character in *Corelli* had also sported a mullet, he was looking forward to bringing back memories of when he and Deb first met. After the hairdresser cut his hair for the role, he snapped a selfie and sent it to Deb, who loved it! But then, the hairdresser continued on with the frosted tips that would complete the character's look, which Deb doesn't like. Darn, the effect was ruined. It's an interesting observation Hugh made at that time, that it had been almost 20 years since his haircuts were based on what he liked, rather than what was needed for an upcoming role.

While his external appearance may have been constantly changing for roles, I love Hugh's 'This is Me' authenticity. He is as goofy as he wants to be, talks with his hands all he wants, and picks projects that sound fun to him. As he says, he spends his career pretending to be other people, so when he's not working, it takes way too much energy to be anything other than his unbridled self!

Hugh's part in the movie took just two weeks of filming, but he had a blast, especially working with Sigourney Weaver. Of course the feeling was mutual. Sigourney said about him, "It's such a pleasure to play with a partner who, whatever direction the scene went in – because Neill let us play around and sort of improvise – he was so game, and he was so talented. Not everyone can do that and not everyone wants to do that."

That's because he approaches his work AS play. We all need a little more of that.

Since he's an optimist by nature, Hugh liked that the story presented artificial intelligence as representing the best parts of humans, unlike a lot of "evil" A.I. stories. And since his character was Australian he got to use his own accent! He said he loves playing a villain, and I suppose that's especially fun when said villain's defeat is filmed by a body double after you've left the country.

They came home by way of Switzerland where Hugh was announced as a new ambassador for Montblanc. They introduced him as "both a style icon and a role model." He mentioned that one thing he was especially excited about was getting to watch the master craftsmen at work. *As someone who's passionate about his own craft, he loves to connect with others who are also devoted to their work.* Montblanc put him right to work filming a commercial called "I Tell Stories." I'd say that's a good fit!

As one project wrapped, several more were announced! Hugh would be on Broadway again at the end of the year in the play, *The River,* and he would play the pirate Blackbeard in the movie *Pan,* to shoot that summer. *Hugh really does choose roles based on what sounds fun.* The director of *Pan*, Joe Wright, recalls how amazed and delighted he was when the movie pitch was sent to Hugh and the response was, "Hugh has always wanted to play a pirate." As for the Broadway play, Hugh was very excited to do a brand new story. He said he and Deb read it aloud together and he was riveted. "I had no idea where it was going. It made me gasp. It moved me."

On February 5, Hugh posted on Instagram that it was "Day one of recording for The Greatest Showman on Earth." When he's IN, he's all-in and things start happening! Pasek and Paul had such a clear vision of the final product that they asked Hugh to get a new vocal teacher that would help him have more of a pop style sound.

At the end of March, Hugh was in London for some promotional appearances building excitement for *Days of Future Past* and to receive the well-deserved Icon Award at the Empire Awards. He joked in his speech that he was really surprised by the recognition, that he "thought this would have happened a lot earlier." Such an adorable dork. The anchor-shaped mustache and beard he was sporting on that tour (trying out possible Blackbeard looks) seemed to bring out his cheeky side, especially on the *Graham Norton Show* with James McAvoy and Michael Fassbender! It's fun to hear him talk about the deeper themes in the X-Men stories. "Every teenager feels like a mutant." *That's a great conversation starter with your teen, by the way. Do they agree with Hugh's statement?*

In April Hugh filmed a few fun things that the public wouldn't find out about until later – a short film for Toyota's Chinese market and his cameo in *Night at the Museum: Secret of the Tomb.* His beard was stunning at that stage, and I think I speak for a lot of fans when I say we would have loved a whole feature-length film of that visage. The Toyota short was called *Levin* (also the name of Hugh's character and of the car it was promoting). Levin says, "I always choose my own path." Hugh liked that line. "I think this is a great quality to have in life." *Freedom is a powerful source of Joy, isn't it?*

In *Night at the Museum,* Hugh reprised his kindergarten role of King Arthur in *Camelot!* I agree with Guinevere, though. His "Wolverine thing" is "better with the claws and no shirt." Hugh likes to tease on Instagram, like his vague April 28, 2014, post of "Monday Morning in a tux" that fans later matched to his scene in the Australian documentary, *That Sugar Film.* One more thing that we wouldn't hear about until later: at a dinner celebrating Jerry Seinfeld's birthday, Hugh asked Jerry how he knew it was the right time to end his TV show. Jerry said it's important not to run yourself dry, but to "leave something in the tank, creatively." That planted the seed in Hugh's mind that he would do one more Wolverine film, then be done.

The *X-Men: Days of Future Past* publicity tour was just about to start when Hugh went back to the doctor for a skin checkup. He was really glad he did because a second basal cell carcinoma spot was discovered. It was just a faint dot and wouldn't have been caught if he hadn't gone in for the routine follow up visit. He has since become very vocal about both protecting yourself from the sun when you're younger, and getting regular checkups as you get older. This is one of the few times in his life

Hugh has looked backward. Since his character in *Days of Future Past* goes back in time, multiple reporters asked what he would do if he personally went back in time. His quick answer: "First thing I'd do is go back and put a little zinc on my nose."

Hugh had a bandaged nose but a big smile at the New York premiere just two days after the surgery, and he was again all smiles at the Beijing and Singapore premieres. At the press conference in Singapore, a reporter asked to speak directly to Wolverine himself. Hugh immediately slipped into character and challenged the reporter to step outside with him, then came back in pretending they'd had a fight. What a crack up! The Australian premiere was in Melbourne on May 16, and of course there were press conferences and other interviews at every stop.

While in Australia, Hugh announced he and Deb were forming the Jackman Furness Foundation for the Performing Arts. The foundation's mission was based on what Kevin Spacey recalled learning from his mentor, Jack Lemon: "When you've had some success, do not forget to send the elevator back down." It was established to support current and future students at Hugh's alma mater, WAAPA.

When you're doing what you love, you can't help but light up others.

At the kickoff event in Perth it was clear in his eyes and his voice how grateful he is for that education. "I would not have gotten where I got if not for what I learned here. I loved it here." And he recalled the most valuable thing he learned: "You're here to try things out, to fall flat on your face, to nurture your talent. You're not here to play safe, you're not here to be 'good,' you're here to learn."

This is how you learn resilience, isn't it? Through having space to try new things, knowing not everything will work, and through celebrating crash-and-burn moments because it means you were forging a new path. When is the last time you felt that freedom to throw caution aside because you knew life would be ok even if you got it wrong?

As the junket went on, lots of reporters wanted details about his nude scene, and his discussion of that on *Live with Kelly and Michael* was pretty hilarious (to wear or not to wear the green-screen sock?). Also while back in New York, he soundly beat Jimmy Fallon in a "cooler scooter" race. Then he made one more trip across the ocean for the premiere in Japan on May 27.

Hosting the Tony Awards again in June, Hugh's hopping Bobby Van tribute was impressive, especially having enough breath to sing at the end! He really does shine in front of a live audience, and my goodness, he made those leading actresses swoon! I like the rapper name LL Cool J gave him, Biggee Tap Shoes. Shortly after the Tonys, the family left to spend the summer in England while Hugh filmed *Pan*.

It feels like Hugh says this about most of his projects, but I think *Pan* really was some of the most fun he ever had on a movie set. The atmosphere was very playful and imaginative. In fact, the director had them do a whole week of pirate boot camp to really get into character. That was when the Nirvana song "Smells Like Teen Spirit" became Hugh's entrance in the film (it wasn't in the script). It takes a competitive high jumper to do that leap up onto the ship's rails, though, especially in that costume! Neverland was the largest set ever built in England up to that point, so it was kind of like a gigantic playground for all the actors, kids and adults! In playing Blackbeard, Hugh drew inspiration from the wicked witch in *The Wizard of Oz*. Scary, but also funny so as not to be relentlessly frightening for kids. He loved the sword fighting scenes (remember his senior year Movement project?) although they were quite a bit trickier than normal up on the mast of the ship! (Fencing on a balance beam, basically!) Rooney Mara commented that Hugh never seemed to get tired in their fight choreography rehearsals. I'm sure that was partly due to his physical condition, but also probably because he was having so much fun! And on weekends, Hugh and family made all of Europe their playground, taking short trips to Paris, Florence, Belgium, and more.

There were several perks about the distinctive look of Hugh's character in *Pan*. One was that they were able to go to Disney World for Ava's birthday and Hugh wasn't recognized at all! Also, he said Deb considered Blackbeard to be the sexiest character he'd ever played, so he recalls 2014 fondly as "a very good summer." On September 1, he showed his beard coming off on Instagram. Bye bye, Blackbeard!

One of the first orders of business back in New York was **the first workshop of the *Greatest Showman* music – when Michael and Hugh met Keala Settle.** Keala was playing Madame Thernardier in *Les Miserables* on Broadway and was recruited by a friend to come in and run through the music. She recalls walking into the room and seeing Hugh Jackman and thinking, "Wait, what is this project??" Hugh heard Keala's accent and asked if she was from New Zealand. When he learned her father was English and her mother was Maori (the indigenous people of New Zealand), he said, "I don't even know you, and I love you." And that set the tone for their relationship. She now calls Hugh her "brother from another mother." Michael recalls that the first moment Keala opened her mouth, he was hooked. I think he cast her as the bearded lady from the beginning, but it took a lot longer for her to see herself in a movie role.

A few days later, Hugh was surprised to learn that Joan Rivers had put in her will that she wanted him sing "Quiet, Please. There's A Lady On Stage" at her funeral. So on September 7, Hugh sang the song Peter Allen wrote for the funeral of his mother-in-law, Judy Garland. Search online for Howard Stern's vivid description of that moving moment.

Leading up to the Global Citizen Festival in Central Park in September, Hugh was once again on *The Tonight Show with Jimmy Fallon* to promote the festival. Jimmy introduced him to the game of pool bowling, and the funniest moment was when Hugh tried to cheat, but accidentally helped Jimmy instead! He pulled one of his own color bowling balls out of the pocket and put it back on the table! During their chat Hugh talked about how Aussie house guests never leave, which gave the producers a hilarious idea, and of course Hugh is always up for a joke. The next day when Jimmy came out for his monologue, Hugh was sleeping on his couch—pillow, blanket, backpack, headphones, pajamas, the whole bit. Jimmy ended up doubled over laughing.

Then Hugh returned to his first love, the stage, starting rehearsals for *The River* on Broadway. His depth of love for his art was evident in an interview, as he described Cush Jumbo's audition.

> *There was a spark, there's a recognition in the eye, of connection. In a way it's an intimacy but really there's a joy. It doesn't matter if you're crying or yelling or screaming or whatever's going on in the scene, you can recognize a joint joy, fun, a feeling of play.*

When you find that kind of mutual enjoyment, definitely find a way to collaborate with those people, whatever industry you're in!

Two different chefs helped Hugh prepare for cleaning and cooking a fish on stage. His family got pretty sick of fish as he practiced, and evidently "a lot of fish guts" were going out in their garbage. Shortly before previews opened, though, he had another skin checkup and had another basal cell carcinoma removed. Opening night of the show was November 16, and Hugh once again auctioned off his shirt after each show, raising another record breaking amount for Broadway Cares Equity Fights AIDS.

Several big milestones happened during the "down time" of the holidays. Laughing Man went big time, becoming distributed by Keurig.

An adorable labradoodle puppy named Allegra joined the Jackman family. (Hugh's Instagram was filled with pictures and videos of the dogs for a while. As a dog lover myself, I say bring it on.) And Taron Egerton came to New York to do a screen test with Hugh for *Eddie the Eagle.* In January, Deb won the New South Wales Australian of the Year award, which she accepted by video.

The River ran through February 8, and shortly after it closed, **the second workshop for the *Greatest Showman* music** was held. Hugh was starting to have doubts again. He told Deb, "I don't know if we're going to get this across the line." He didn't feel like the studio was catching the vision that he and Michael had. Deb said, "Stop. You're either going to believe in this fully and make it happen or you've got to step away." He listened to her, of course, and that very night, he started visualizing the movie being a big hit, and changing people's lives, particularly kids' lives. He made it part of his routine every night to visualize it.

We're still seeing the results of that visualization every day on Twitter—videos of kids singing and dancing to the soundtrack.

In mid-February Hugh did publicity for *Chappie* around the world. Then on March 2, Hugh recalls waking up from a sound sleep at 4:00 a.m. with a clear idea for the movie that would become *Logan.* He recorded a voice memo describing his vision and sent it to James Mangold.

Eddie the Eagle was filmed primarily in Bavaria. Hugh's character depends on alcohol as his "jacket," so he filmed most of the movie, up in the snowy mountains, with no coat. "I was freezing that entire movie! FREEZING!" he said. And Hugh is usually a bit of a daredevil, game for anything, but he said when they went to the top of the 90 meter ski jump to film, he thought, "There is absolutely no way in hell I would do this." But he loved working with Taron. Hugh's dialect coach, with whom he's worked on more than 20 movies, commented, "I've never seen you laugh so much on a film! It seems you had more fun on this film than ever!" And Dexter Fletcher, the director, agreed. "It was difficult, because we're trying to do a serious job and we just laughed so much." And he gave very sweet insight into the relationship between his two leads. "Taron wanted to impress Hugh, and Hugh was impressed." A few little "outtakes" of Hugh laughing uproariously at Taron would make it into the final movie.

In mid-March, while he wasn't needed on set, he went to Istanbul for another iteration of his one-man show. He did press interviews and rehearsals, but his voice was not feeling healthy. Wisely, he got checked out by a doctor who said that he had a vocal hemorrhage, and he needed to rest his voice or he was in danger of doing permanent damage. So he had to cancel those performances, but he promised to return to Istanbul when he could. *Listening to your body is always a good idea.*

On March 28, he announced via Instagram that he would be doing one final Wolverine film, so the conversations with James Mangold about his idea must have been going well! The studio portions of *Eddie the Eagle* were filmed in London, then Hugh was home by mid-April. Hugh dives intensely into work, but has also gotten good at down time and family time. He did lots of beach walking with the dogs in the Hamptons, took the family to Hawaii, and saw *Hamilton* when it was still off-Broadway.

Remember to refill your cup.

On May 9, he completed the lifts that qualified him for the 1,000 pound club at the Dogpound: 355 Squat, 235 Bench, and 410 Deadlift. *How is he able to achieve feats like that? His Want Engine (he loves the feeling of being strong and the routine of working out regularly) and his Belief Engine (believing he can do it and having others believe in him as well) are both powering in the same direction.* At the end of the month, he was feeling healthy enough to go back to Istanbul to make up the shows he had canceled earlier.

Hugh has mentioned a couple times that he appreciated the joy on the *Eddie the Eagle* set all the more because it was during a difficult time for him personally. He hasn't elaborated, other than to credit producer Matthew Vaughn with strengthening his confidence that it's healthy for family to take precedence over career. We know Hugh and Deb made that determination from the beginning as it pertained to each other and their kids, so it seems he and Deb might have been expanding that framework to include aging parents. Based on his decision not to play the lead in *Collateral Beauty,* and pushing back the timeline of other projects in order to spend more time in Australia, I'd say they did well making use of precious time.

I talk about this often with my team. When you're in a business you're passionate about and momentum is building, balance with family can be tricky. The healthiest path seems to be recognizing that there are phases. There are times when your family rallies to support a focus on business, and times when the business might need to slow down a little so family can be the focus. The only "rule" is to have your head and heart connected so you can adjust your focus as you go.

Spending that summer back in Australia I guess makes it "that winter." There were big things happening with Adopt Change. As they were starting to make headway with policy and political leaders, it was important to Deb to also make sure best practices and systems were developed to support adoptive families. Hugh made a quick trip back to San Diego in July for Comic-Con, promoting *Pan* and talking about the final Wolverine film (he briefly crashed the *X-Men Apocalypse* panel and plopped on Jennifer Lawrence's lap).

In August, Deb spent some time doing press interviews and visiting schools as Australian of the Year. She mentioned that she was open to acting roles since their kids were getting older, including Australian productions, but hadn't found the right one yet. She asked writers to create more strong, positive older female characters! (Stay tuned.)

From the number of old photos and mementos Hugh posted on Instagram that winter, he must have been going through boxes from his childhood. While enjoying the family time, Hugh was also gearing up to announce his next adventure, turning his one-man show into an arena spectacular – touring Australia with *Broadway to Oz*. As he said with an enormous grin just before walking on stage to make the announcement, "I'm about to tick off a big one from my bucket list." He talked to his agent about bringing the arena show to the US, but at that point, Patrick didn't think it would have the draw needed to succeed outside Australia. (Again, stay tuned.)

Since Deb had gotten Adopt Change up and running in Australia, some child advocates she had connected with in New York wanted her to bring her energy and ability to get things done to the US as well. There was a lot of interest in tackling the root causes of why there are so many kids without a permanent family in the first place! She brought together passionate people to discuss how to have the biggest impact, and started putting together the board of a new organization they called Hopeland. She hadn't found the right person to be the CEO until Hugh Evans, founder of Global Citizen, suggested she talk to his brother. She met Nick Evans in England where he lived, and after talking for a couple of hours, she convinced him to move to New York to take the job!

On a podcast interview she was asked about the "gravitational force" of her work, how she "pulled into the cause some of the most powerful and passionate people in the world," like presidents, prime ministers, philanthropists, Hollywood A-listers, and rock stars. Deb is matter-of-fact about it. "Those are the people who CAN make a difference!"

Deb always believes there IS a solution, and that's where she focuses. Get to the root of any issue, and start moving in a better direction. Her vision is so strong, and her belief that things can get better is so powerful, people can't help but jump on board.

Back to the movie business, the press junket for *Pan* started in Melbourne, which allowed Hugh and Deb to celebrate the 20th anniversary of their engagement by attending the Red Ball for the Fight Cancer Foundation. They were home in New York for about a week (time to reunite with those beloved dogs!), then made trips to London and Paris for *Pan* premieres. All the while Hugh continued to work out, preparing for his final stint as Wolverine.

In interviews during that time, you get a sense of what putting on the claws for the last time meant to him. "I'm trying to do something with this that is a little special, a little different. I've got a very, very strong idea of what that is. I really have known for quite a long time how I want to finish this sort of odyssey that I've been on, this amazing journey. And I won't let it fall anywhere in between. I won't fall short of that." His feelings were so strong that he wasn't going to start shooting until he felt like the script REALLY captured the depth he was looking for. "I'm pushing harder than I ever have before. People ask me 'How are you going to be able to let it go?' To me the only way you can let it go is if you've just left blood every day on that studio floor." We know he's referring to his level of intensity and commitment, but turns out it's kind of literal, too...

Remember, Joy doesn't mean always easy and relaxed. It means something different for each of us, and it means different things on different days. The key is to follow YOUR own joy, because that leads you into the fullness of who you are.

Hugh was actually a little surprised that the studio approved the movie he and James Mangold wanted to make. "We were trying to do something that was different from all the other *X-Men* movies." *The key is, their vision was CLEAR. And that gave the studio confidence to say yes.* Hugh later commented that he had figured out a new formula for making a project happen. "It actually takes less people than you think, who believe more, who fight harder." *I agree. To paraphrase Margaret Mead, a small group of people with focus and passion can accomplish astounding things.*

Back in New York, Hugh hosted the Global Citizen Festival once again, this time with co-host Stephen Colbert. They opened the show with Stephen on Hugh's shoulders in a long trench coat. Stephen said he was initially worried about hurting Hugh, but actually his legs hurt after sitting on Hugh's muscular shoulders! Hugh later told the story that it was while they were on stage that he realized his eyesight was getting bad enough again (he'd had Lasik eye surgery earlier) that he couldn't read what he was supposed to be announcing, so Stephen picked up the slack. Hugh got contacts again after that!

The beginning of October found Hugh back in Australia starting rehearsals for *Broadway to Oz*. The final dress rehearsal was November 23, opening night was November 24, and from there it was a whirlwind three weeks around Australia. Russell Crowe joined in the December 2 performance. The audiences loved the show, and Hugh loved entertaining thousands of home-country fans. *Joy and happiness all around.*

After wrapping up the tour, they had more down time with family and friends. Hugh was spotted in Sorrento by someone who reported: "Nothing like Hugh Jackman at Christmas Eve mass to brighten things up. Strategic move from the Catholic Church getting him to do the collection. The ladies couldn't get the money in the basket fast enough!"

See? Joy is a powerful motivator! ☺

Then once again, their travel makes my head spin. After New Year's, the family flew back to New York from Australia. On January 13 Hugh took a quick two-day trip to Budapest for a Montblanc shoot, then flew back to New York. A few days later he again flew to Europe to attend an event in Geneva, flying back to New York the next day. A week later he and Deb went to Utah for a "surprise screening" of *Eddie the Eagle* at the Sundance Film Festival, then on to Los Angeles for the G'Day USA Gala and some press interviews. Hugh and Taron Egerton appeared on *The Ellen Show* – Taron's first US talk show. Hugh was back in New York by the end of the month. Folks wondered about the beard he was starting to grow, which they later found out was for his *X-Men Apocalypse* cameo.

The *Eddie the Eagle* press tour seemed to be filled with constant laughter, and it was undeniable how much Hugh and Taron enjoyed each other's company. As much fun as they had making the movie, I think they had even more fun traveling to promote it, judging by moments like their striking a Saturday Night Fever pose as the curtain went up on Steve Harvey's show. And they were both extremely proud of the film. Hugh said, "It's so great to be part of something that makes people happy, that I can show my kids, too." Taron said his dream for the movie would be for it to be shown on TV on Christmas Day. Except Michael Gracey was having the same dream about the project he was working on...

The final workshop of *The Greatest Showman* was scheduled for February 9 in New York, at which they hoped to get the film greenlit. It had taken eight months to find a date that worked for everyone who needed to be there. Studio executives and financers were flying in from around the world to hear the music and the story. On February 8, Hugh went in for another routine skin checkup while he was home, and they found another spot which needed to be removed immediately.

After stitching him up, the doctor asked Hugh if he'd be able to relax for a few days, and Hugh told him about the workshop the next day. The doctor said he absolutely could not sing, or he would risk ripping the stitches and the wound could get infected. You've probably seen the video of how that went. (If not, stop and Google it right now.) For most of the day, Hugh did what the doctor said. He spoke the lines, he acted the part, but Jeremy Jordan filled in the singing for his role. However, in the final musical number, "From Now On," Hugh just couldn't hold back. As many times as I've seen that video, it continues to give me goosebumps every time. The executives felt the magic that day, which is good because Hugh and Michael had already been moving forward with planning pre-production to start about a month later, Michael says, "We were just going. We were just believing." Oh, and Hugh DID have to go back to the surgeon and have the stitches redone!

But that wasn't the only magical moment that day. **We watch *The Greatest Showman* now and think, "Of course Keala is the bearded lady! Who else could it be?" But it wasn't always that clear.** Some big names were pursuing the role. At that final workshop, the 'will we or won't we' decision point, Keala didn't want the pressure of singing "This is Me." The song had just been written so had only been heard in rehearsal, but Hugh, Michael, and the other performers already knew it would become the anthem of the film. Michael had to bribe her with a bottle of Jameson to get her to agree to the solo. In the rehearsal he kept encouraging her to step out from behind the music stand into the middle of the room, but she wouldn't. Finally, in the actual workshop, with her hands and voice shaking, she did. She looked over at Hugh as she sang the words "I am who I'm meant to be, this is me" for the first time in public, and seemed to gather courage from him. As she sang the next line, "Look out 'cause here I come…" she slowly moved the stand aside and stepped forward. Goosebumps.

Keala said, "I had to face a lot of demons to get that song out." If you haven't seen the video of that electric moment, stop reading and watch that, too. At the end of that song (it wasn't the end of the show, mind you, it was in the middle of the workshop), the studio head rushed over to give

Keala a hug and whispered in her ear, "You just booked your first major motion picture."

I think Hugh was still flying high after the excitement of that workshop, and as the *Eddie the Eagle* press tour continued, he reminded us *Eddie* was a Joy Revolution story, too.

> *What I love about this story is it's a crazy dream that he had. No one in Britain had jumped I think since 1927. And I think everybody harbors some [crazy dream], if you get people with their guards down and say 'If you could do anything, what is it you really want to do?' Most people don't allow themselves to follow that through, it's just like a 'wish' thing. But Eddie's an example of 'No, I'm going to do it!' Even when people were laughing at him, when people were telling him not to do it, he just was like, 'No, this is the only thing I love.'*

They got to do some pretty cool things on that press tour, like indoor skydiving; and Hugh got a chance to ride in an F16 fighter jet. Taron declined that particular opportunity, and Hugh was grateful that he didn't get sick during the flight. At the end of February he snuck in a quick trip to Montreal to film his *Apocalypse* scene. March brought premieres in Korea, China, Norway, England, Germany, and France, finishing in Australia. Those childhood dreams of traveling the world sure came out bigger than he ever could have imagined, didn't they?

On the *Jonathan Ross Show,* Jonathan asked Hugh about his famous When-Harry-Met-Sally-like scene. Hugh shared that Deb wasn't sold on his acting in that part. When she saw the film for the first time, she leaned over and said to him, "It doesn't look anything like that." He also shared that the final Wolverine movie would start shooting "pretty soon."

At the beach in Sydney there was a riptide scare and Hugh helped several people to safety. Of course the news led with the actions of their "real-life superhero!" But Hugh minimized the drama. "Any dad would do the same thing, anyone would do the same thing. There were other people out there helping people in." As far as superhero status, he laughed. "Claws don't help in the water." But yes, it helps that he was close to shooting another superhero movie, so was pretty damn strong.

In April Deb and Hugh got away for a romantic trip to St. Bart's celebrating their 20th anniversary. "We want to relive our honeymoon,"

Hugh said. It's good they got that time to relax, because the rest of the year would be PACKED!

CHAPTER 9

GOODBYE WOLVERINE, HELLO REVOLUTION!

Hugh and Deb's schedule always makes my jaw drop, but it was particularly full in the middle of 2016. A lot of exciting things were happening, so it's a good thing they both love to be on the go!

Right after they got back from their anniversary trip, Deb announced that she would be returning to Australian TV, playing the role of Claudia Rossini, Director of Counterterrorism, Australian Security Intelligence Organization, on *Hyde and Seek*. It may have been a bit earlier than she intended to return to work, especially since it was already a busy year with Hugh filming *Logan,* so they would be breaking their "only one of us works at a time" rule, but she loved the role. Her character was "a tough, intelligent, politically-minded woman who works in a top Government security role and knows how to get what she wants," much better than the usual roles for women past 40. Other roles for middle-aged women mostly depicted depressed, regretful people which she pointed out was "not overly challenging or exciting to tackle." But she loved playing this "sassy, interesting, and smart" woman in a thriller! People were so excited to see her on screen again!

Deb had commented previously that sometimes she would get sent a script and she'd rather play one of the male roles because they were much more developed characters, and she would voice that frustration! She wasn't sure anyone was listening, but I think by holding out for more interesting roles for older women, Deb had a part in manifesting them in the industry. The role of Claudia was particularly significant in the political action thriller genre, often dominated by male characters. Deb said more scripts were needed representing interesting women past 40, because "that's when women are particularly interesting." *Intriguing thought, isn't it? It's certainly true for me, coming out of the time-consuming and intense stage of raising small children, I'm doing things I never imagined, like running a nationwide business from my laptop, becoming a leader in my community, and writing this book.*

A few days after Deb's announcement, **Fox confirmed at CinemaCon in Las Vegas that *The Greatest Showman* movie was a go.** In late April, Daniel Campos posted a video about giving Hugh a private dance lesson. Campos, known as Cloud in the dance world, would become the assistant choreographer on *The Greatest Showman* and would play the unusually rhythmically talented bartender in "The Other Side" scene.

While in the final stages of growing the mutton chops and bulking up to Wolverine size for the last time, Hugh spent some quality time in a studio with a microphone, recording the voice of Sir Lionel Frost in the stop-motion animation feature *Missing Link* with Laika studios. It's hard to imagine how one more thing could have been squeezed in, but when Barbra Streisand emailed that she'd like Hugh to sing "Any Moment Now" on her collaboration album, he found a way. She is one of Deb's favorite singers, so Deb was incredibly excited to have Hugh record with her. Barbra chose Hugh because of his ability to act through song, and indeed, the final version, including their spoken dialogue, is such an accurate portrayal of how communication can go wrong in a relationship and cause people to drift apart, it's painful to listen to. *Knowing my husband and I have been there, I'm so thankful we found our way back to each other! More on that in chapter 12.*

Deb was shooting in Australia and Hugh left to start filming in the southwestern US. Who knows how they managed their "never apart more than two weeks" rule during this time! But as always, it had been a joint decision. "He's very supportive and was thrilled I took this on," Deborralee told *TV Week*. She said she was "in and out" of the show because she was back in the US a lot also. "They accommodated me because I was like 'My kids are at school in New York.' They shot me in the time I had in Australia." At first it felt scary, and she remembers thinking "Damn, do I remember how to do this?" It was her first role in about five years, and I know many people who have taken time away from a full-time career to focus on kids can relate. But it was like riding a bike. As a co-star said, "She killed it."

Any mom returning to a previous profession might feel rusty, but it doesn't take long to figure out that you've honed valuable problem solving and project management and conflict resolution skills as a parent! And she had a blast. "Getting my creative juices flowing has felt fantastic," she said. The character fit her like a glove. "I'm like that – I believe in justice, and I'm outspoken in what I think is right and wrong." Co-star Emma Hamilton said, "Her character had us all shaking in our boots."

For Hugh, portraying Wolverine for the last time was quite an emotional journey. "It's a deeply personal film. I felt it was important to really see the Wolverine that I knew and felt and had gotten to know over 17 years. So I would have done anything, but I was stubborn, too."

It was a warm summer in Louisiana and New Mexico. The production kept a pretty tight lid on filming news, but one tidbit that leaked was that Patrick Stewart was allegedly better at ping pong than Hugh. Some of the scenes they filmed were at high altitude, and Hugh was still in the habit of pushing himself a little too hard. On one take, when he found himself flat on the ground, he said, "Let's do it again. I tripped." The camera man replied, "No. You passed out."

Once again I have no doubt Hugh brings out the best in any child actor he works with. I love how he talked about Dafne Keen, especially how crazy it was to watch her play with his daughter at a water park on the weekend, then have her on set on Monday "scaring the crap out of me!"

While they were filming, **progress continued on *Showman***. In mid-June, Zac Efron officially joined the cast. Later that month Michael Gracey presented about the film at CineEurope, calling it "a return to the classic film musical" similar to *Mary Poppins* and *The Sound of Music*. People listening may have thought his vision was a little lofty. *As we now know, his vision was spot on.* In early July it was announced that Michelle Williams was on board, although at that point people speculated she would be playing the part of Jenny Lind, not of Charity Barnum.

On August 22, Hugh shaved off the mutton chops for the last time. *Geek Culture* asked Hugh how he felt the last day on set as Logan. "It was calm— a good feeling. I knew I'd made the right decision."

As Hugh wrapped up a movie about mortality and family, Deb's mother transitioned from this world. Deb was in Melbourne with her for the last few weeks before she died on August 27. Growing up as the only child of a single mother, it would be hard to overstate how much of an impact it had on Deb to have her mum's physical journey come to an end. Hugh was very close to Fay as well. As Deb adjusted to life without her mum's physical presence, she spent some time slowing down and focusing on creative projects like painting and writing.

What a beautiful example of self-care, a way to honor Fay's lasting influence.

When they returned from Australia to New York, **rehearsals and soundtrack recording sessions for *Showman* started. The long-dreamt-about, eight-years-in-development project was coming to fruition!** And rehearsals were intense! Zendaya was learning to be a trapeze artist, and they were all learning complicated choreography. Hugh's description: "We worked really hard, and then we would work on weekends, and I loved it!" As demanding as *Logan* was to film, Hugh says *Showman* was even more difficult physically.

Why were they all excited about working so hard? Why was Zac so persistent about getting to do a knee slide when it's both tricky and painful? When you admire someone's "work ethic," what you're really seeing is someone doing what they love. That's the secret sauce.

Keala described it like this:

> *When you have your number one person on that call sheet that comes in every day, no matter what, at 500 miles per hour, ready to go, and grabbing the hands of everybody that is around him to say 'and I want you to come with me because I know you can, that's why I wanted you on this project,' you can't say no to that.*

The hat tricks Hugh incorporated into his scenes were paying homage to Donald O'Connor's performance of "Make 'Em Laugh" in *Singing in the Rain,* Hugh's favorite movie of all time. It's hard for me to choose a favorite scene from *Showman*, but if I had to narrow it down it would be Barnum and Charity's dance on the rooftop. It looks so graceful and effortless, when it was anything but. "There are big lifts, and Michelle's tall. It's beautiful, but it's actually quite athletic as well," Ashley Wallen, the choreographer, said.

Even during a movie shoot, their schedule is full. Hugh again hosted the Global Citizen Festival on Sept 24, and the following weekend he went to Los Angeles to perform at the Motion Picture Television Fund's 95th anniversary celebration, while Deb went to Australia to do publicity for *Hyde and Seek.* Hugh was on set rehearsing on his 48th birthday. As a surprise, they brought in a very colorfully dressed drum line for a fitting celebration. Hugh even got to take a turn on the drum set! But what he wanted most for his birthday was to climb a mountain, so the family went to Utah for a weekend. Deb doesn't like heights but said she did it for the kids, to show them she was doing it in spite of her fear. I'm not sure the kids really needed her example, though, as she said they were fearless! *Maybe a better description is that the kids gave Deb the encouragement she needed to expand her comfort zone.* She described a suspension bridge they crossed that I don't have any desire to add to my comfort zone in the foreseeable future!

Two weeks before they started filming (so they had already been rehearsing for eight weeks), Hugh got a letter from the studio saying that since the project was now greenlit, he couldn't ride his bike to rehearsal anymore. The studio underlined the part about the bike, thinking that was the most important part of the message. But the part that was most crucial to Hugh was, "Wait, we have only just now been officially greenlit??" *My takeaway is that when momentum is strong, you don't necessarily have to wait for official permission.* Filming began November 22. Hugh spent a little time in California in December doing reshoots for *Logan,* then in February of 2017, he had another skin checkup and another basal cell carcinoma spot was removed.

A journalist asked Michael Gracey when he knew the film was something magical. My answer would be that he saw the vision of the magic eight years before, and that's why it turned out the way it did. But Michael's answer was good, too. He said the feeling on set was often magical. Other actors who weren't in the scene would be there to cheer on their colleagues, clapping and shouting behind the monitors. He saw a glow in the actors' eyes through the camera, and felt an electricity on the set.

As has happened several times in his career, in the middle of filming one movie, Hugh had to take a hiatus to do press for another. The world premiere of *Logan* was on February 17 at the Berlin Film Festival. Hugh described *Logan* as the story of "a man who's terrified of love and intimacy being surrounded by family." It's very touching to hear Hugh and Patrick describe watching the premiere together. At this point I think I'm safe sharing the spoiler that both of their characters die in the movie, but probably what made this an emotional night for them is seeing on screen a depth of relationship between their two characters that hadn't been seen before. And I'm sure it was sinking in that this was the end of 17 years of working together in those roles. As the final scene played, Hugh reached over and took Patrick's hand, and they were both wiping away tears. (Hugh joked about James Mangold on the other side of him saying, "Get it together! You're Wolverine!")

In *Logan,* Hugh and James Mangold wanted to first and foremost make a really good movie. And Hugh wanted to really dig into the depth of the character, to explore the dark corners of his complexity. X-Men stories have always had a deeper meaning, originally representing the civil rights movement (Professor Xavier represents Dr. Martin Luther King, Jr. and Magneto represents Malcom X.) But *Logan* has a message about the aftermath of violence that hadn't been seen before in comic book movies. It also explores "humanity and connection and family." Yes, Hugh. We love that about the projects you choose, and we love how you manifest your characters' complex humanness.

After Berlin there were once again premieres and TV appearances all over the world. On the *Graham Norton Show,* Hugh and Patrick were paid a surprise visit by Ian McKellen. See if you can find a video of that show – even after multiple watchings it brings me some most delightful belly laughs!

Anytime Hugh wasn't traveling, he was in New York filming *Showman.* On March 2, he did several talk show appearances for *Logan.* That night, they filmed all night—the scene of the circus burning down, and then the following day there were more press interviews. I'm not really sure when he slept, maybe on the plane to China the next day. They did a lot of the night shoots toward the end of the process, presumably so it would be a little bit warmer, although Keala recalls that it was absolutely freezing the night they filmed the outdoor portion of "This Is Me." On April 6, which happened to be my 45th birthday, *The Greatest Showman* wrapped. Hugh gave gifts to the cast along with a note that gives me goosebumps. "This film is a 7-year dream come true. Thank you from the bottom of my heart for helping to realize this dream. Love, Hugh." Then he and Deb went on a vacation to Tahiti.

Hugh did more promotion for *Logan* in May, including the MTV Movie and TV Awards on May 7, where he and Daphne won best duo. Their acceptance speech is one of the best ever. At the end of May, Hugh was in Japan for the premiere there.

The family spent most of that summer traveling to Greece and Italy, and then to Australia, but it wasn't all relaxation. Hugh was working his way through stacks of research binders about Gary Hart, and watching hours and hours of footage, preparing to film *The Front Runner.* And Deb did some press for the screening of a restored version of *Shame* at the

Melbourne International Film Festival, 29 years after it was released. Deb was looking forward to having their kids, especially their daughter, see the film. "I love that she gets to watch Mum kick some ass, to see a strong female. [Asta] was a great role model for a lot of young girls."

When they returned to the US, Hugh dove back into research, spending a few days with Gary Hart and his family. Is there a more in-depth level of research than staying in the subject's home, even sleeping in his bedroom and hanging your clothes in his closet? (Gary and Lee Hart were sleeping on the main level of the house while Lee recovered from surgery, so they put Hugh in the master bedroom upstairs.) When he returned to New York, he and Deb co-hosted another Global Citizen Festival.

Global Citizen, founded by Hugh Evans with the Jackmans' support from the beginning, is another organization that embodies the Joy Revolution. Ending extreme poverty in the world by 2030 is an ambitious goal and wouldn't be possible without a founder who strongly believes in that dream and stays focused on solutions – on what CAN be done. *When you dream crazy dreams and are open to ideas that no one has even imagined before, big things happen!* Hugh (J) describes Hugh Evans as a disruptor, someone whose vision isn't limited by what's been done before (similar to P.T. Barnum). Deb said about the Festival, "I love that we come together in Joy, not as angry citizens, but through music. We're brought here to discuss the issues *and* share something beautiful." It creates a crowd of people taking action driven by hope!

In mid-September Hugh left for Atlanta to start filming *The Front Runner*. This new project provided another opportunity to do something he had never done before: play a living person whom he had met, and who would ultimately watch his performance.

Do you see how a comfort zone gets expanded? You start with a foundation of something you are already confident in, see a new challenge that excites you, prepare as best you can, take a few deep breaths, visualize the best possible outcome, then step into the new adventure!

During filming, the cast did a full reading of the script of *The Princess Bride* as a fundraiser for Puerto Rico after Hurricane Maria. Evidently the first time Hugh said, "As you wish," the crowd went nuts. I'm guessing it wasn't video or audio recorded for copyright reasons, so I'll just have to watch it in my imagination.

Promotion of *The Greatest Showman* kicked off with Hugh adding a golden deer to his awards shelf, receiving the Bambi Award for Entertainment in Berlin. In December he was back in Europe for more promotional appearances, including being honored by BAFTA with A Life in Pictures, or as he said, "Can we call it a Half Life? I'm not done yet!" On December 6, he and Zac and Zendaya filmed the *Graham Norton Show* that would air on New Year's Eve. (It was so much fun to watch them stutter when Graham asked what they got for Christmas! Hugh was quickest on his feet, and he gets how manifesting works! "Zac gave me a car!") A few days later, the glamorous work of promoting a film took them to a freezing sidewalk in Manhattan where they taped *Crosswalk the Musical* with James Corden. That night was the world premiere aboard the Queen Mary, docked in New York City, and the next day the Empire State Building was lit up in celebration of *The Greatest Showman*. On the 11th, Golden Globe nominations were announced, including nods for the film, for Hugh, and for the song, "This is Me."

After a quick trip to Mexico for the premiere there, they went to Los Angeles to prepare for the live commercial during *A Christmas Story* on December 17. What a high pressure event – singing, dancing, and doing hat tricks in a live (and very expensive) TV commercial! Good thing Hugh loves intensity.

Joshua Simon from YAAAS TV asked Hugh what 2017 had taught him.

> *Follow your gut. Take risks. And be authentic, be who you are. I have a theory of life that you can always sleep peacefully at night, even if something fails, if you follow your gut, if you believe in it. If it doesn't catch on you can go, 'OK, well maybe I was wrong or maybe I'm the only one in the world who liked it, but it was right for me.'*

Count me in for that approach to life.

On December 20, *The Greatest Showman* was released in the US Critics hadn't been impressed, and it didn't open with a bang. In fact, it was the second worst box office result of movies that opened in wide release around that time. **But Deb said, "It's gonna happen. I feel it. Don't worry."** And what has happened since is the kind of story Barnum himself would have eaten up. On December 23, my daughter and I went to the movie with her teachers at Iowa Circus Arts. And like millions of others around the world, we fell in love. And also like millions of others around the world, we downloaded the soundtrack in the parking lot of the movie theater as we left.

The movie isn't meant to be a factual biopic of Barnum. As Hugh explained, "It uses his story to make us see the positivity in life, that life is what you choose to make it, and that we should be embracing people who are left on the outside." Jess Cagle of *People Magazine* asked Hugh what it was about Barnum's story that he most identified with, recognizing that a big part of the story is Barnum "juggling having a family and chasing those dreams [of show business]." Even as Jess asked the question, Hugh unconsciously started fiddling with his wedding ring. "Finding a balance in life, I would still say, is the great art for all of us. Getting that balance right, as a father, as a husband, for yourself, for your work, is tough. So for me, that's something Deb and I are always talking about."

I don't think there's any such thing as a perfect balance, but talking about it is success. I certainly have days where things feel out of whack. The quickest way back for me is to sit down with a notebook and write out my priorities, starting with myself and my health (my own oxygen mask), then my immediate family, then whatever else is high on the list. Then with my autopilot brain refocused, I can move forward doing what I feel a pull toward in the moment.

They did well regarding balance by spending the 2017 holidays in Australia with family and a group of friends who came to visit them down under! Keala sang at Carols by Candlelight in Melbourne on Christmas Eve (Hugh and Deb were there cheering her on!) then she joined them for Christmas dinner. (Awww.) It's good that Hugh had a lot of fun things happening personally, since the initial numbers from the film's opening were pretty depressing.

Then in January, things started to shift. The soundtrack was selling very well! In fact, Hugh told Ellen DeGeneres on January 5 that he had a dream to have an album in a frame. (By May he would be holding his framed platinum record.) Box office numbers started going UP each weekend. That doesn't happen with movies – opening weekend "always" brings in the biggest numbers then it goes down from there. Not so with *The Greatest Showman*. People, like my daughter and I, were deeply touched by the movie and spread the word – to relatives, on social media, at playdates, at the office water cooler... By mid-January when things were really cooking, promoting the film in Europe was probably a lot more fun! They went from Paris to Tokyo, where everyone adores Hugh, then back to London, where *Showman* became a bona fide cultural phenomenon.

As of this writing, the film brought in almost half a billion dollars at the box office, it's the third highest grossing movie musical EVER, and its soundtrack was 2018's top selling album around the world. Not top selling movie soundtrack, top selling ALBUM. Of all albums. In the WORLD. What a revolution! AND it earned Hugh a Grammy!

In March, Hugh was in London for the Empire Awards, where he won a well-deserved Best Actor award for *Logan*. I love that the sound team chose the song "There Goes My Hero" for his walking music.

In April 2018 Deb was honored with a Disruptor Award at the Tribeca Innovation Awards in New York. "I used to get detention for being disruptive. Now they give me an award!" she said as she walked up to the microphone to accept it.

Reading about that award, on top of hearing Hugh describe Barnum as a disruptor during Showman press, I am proudly claiming the disruptor label. We can't solve problems using the same thinking that created them. (That statement is often attributed to Einstein, but what he actually wrote was "a new type of thinking is essential if mankind is to survive and move toward higher levels.") My version is, we don't solve problems by focusing on the problem. We change the world by expanding our dreams of what's possible and moving toward them.

In August Deb announced a huge milestone in Australia, a Parliamentary Friends of Adoption coalition. What a culture change from when she started, when talking about adoption was taboo among policy makers! Adopt Change is thriving in Australia more than she could have imagined when she first spoke out. She told Jenny Cooney on the *Aussies in Hollywood* podcast in September 2018, "We've got an office in Sydney, we've got 20 staff, and we're really making a shift. Children are getting out of foster care that have been stuck there for years and years, so that is thrilling."

What's next for Deb? "I still have that passion that I do want to direct." Asked if she and Hugh would like to work together, her response was, "I'm looking forward to auditioning him." Never a dull moment with those two! Hugh credits Deb with manifesting many milestones in his career, and now he's returning the favor. The picture he paints is, "She's writing, reading, getting ready to direct her Oscar-winning film."

So while Hugh is in increasingly high demand for dramatic movie roles, as it seems some people are just now discovering there's more to him than Wolverine, why would he take a year off from movies to do a worldwide concert tour? As he told *WAtoday,*

146

It feels like a privilege; I was really excited to basically give the year up for it. I'm at a point in my career where I don't worry about that stuff: momentum, trajectory, or what people think. I really sort of march to the beat of my own drummer now, and I don't think I've always been like that."

From my observation, it appears that he has always followed his gut, but it makes sense that he hasn't always been able to do so with such confidence. And now? I can't wait to see what he does with his next 50 years, can you? I am going to thoroughly enjoy continuing to watch and learn from Hugh and Deb in the coming years!

PART III
YOUR JOY REVOLUTION

CHAPTER 10

WILD THING...

Do more of what makes your heart sing.

Everyone finds joy in different things. Some find it in nature. Some find it in testing the limits of their body. Some find it in scouring through computer code to find a miniscule error. Some find it in sitting with individuals on their deathbed. Some find it in sorting laundry. Some find it in creating delicious food. One person's joy can be another's nightmare. That's why it's important for you to find what opens YOUR soul.

Hugh said about acting, "I firmly believe art's job is to melt the hearts of the audience. Therefore, as a performer, your job is to open yourself up. You have to be truthful. Of course we're pretending, of course I'm not P.T. Barnum, but on some level, me, Hugh Jackman, you have to rip your heart open. And in that moment, when an audience is there to receive it, you're connected. It is so powerful, and it can last a lifetime."

In another interview he took that description even further to describe the pinnacle of what he's felt on stage:

> *It's almost a slightly out of body experience. You can stand on stage with 2000 strangers and feel like you know them intimately and they know you intimately, and feel completely safe. You can open up your heart, and they're opening up their hearts, and you're completely connected. It's in that instant a feeling of absolute privilege, that you can experience it, and so powerful that it raises the hairs on the back of your neck.*

He clarified that it's not something you can force, it has to come from within you. He talks about tap dancing in a similar way. If he gets up early on a holiday, Deb might suggest that he take the day off, then she remembers that dancing in the early morning isn't work to him, it's soul food.

What part of your life gives you that feeling? If nothing at the moment, can you think back on things you've enjoyed in the past that you could make time for again? Or what's that thing you've always wanted to try? Do it! It could open up a whole new side of you, or give you a new zest for life! Keep following what sounds fun.

Hugh also finds a lot of joy in sports—following his favorite teams in detail and attending as many events as possible. Deb and their kids don't share that same interest, and that's fine! Refer to Chapter 13: Let other people be who they are. In our 17 years of marriage, my husband has always let me know whether the Chicago Cubs won or lost that day. And after 17 years, I still don't really care. But I enjoy hearing about it because it matters to him. Recently I've started responding by letting him know what's new that day in Hugh's world, or showing him a photo of what Hugh was wearing the day before. (Dave is picking up some great style tips!) That's the same, right? A fan is a fan!

What makes *my* heart sing? Music opens my soul. You'll recall that the first thing I Googled after seeing *The Greatest Showman* was if it was actually Hugh singing. I wanted to know because the singing moved me in a powerful way. The first thing that came up in my search was the video of the workshop where the movie was greenlit. You know, the one where Hugh's doctor had forbidden him to sing because of the skin cancer surgery the previous day, and he made it through most of the story letting someone else sing for him, but when they got to "From Now On" he couldn't hold back. In his words, "I thought, 'I'll sing the first line.' It was [soft and low]. 'Ah, I'll sing the second line.' And then the music just took over." Watching that video, I got goosebumps. Seeing Hugh so moved by the music, and able to create such emotion through it, was intoxicating.

I'm not kidding about music laying my heart open. I've stopped playing in the pit orchestra for musicals and operas because even without seeing what was happening on stage, I always fell in love with the leading man. Instrumentalists, too! Have you seen that scene in *Impromptu* where the woman lies under the piano to feel the vibrations in her body as Chopin plays? Yep, I've done that.

So what makes music create transcendence for me? I think Hugh nails it, "Something about singing—it makes you breathe, makes you open up, it makes you vulnerable. You have to be free, in a way, to sing." Creating clear vibrations with an instrument requires a similar openness.

It's interesting that Hugh says he hasn't been a confident singer for a lot of his career. He feels most confident as an actor, which I understand, as that's what his training was. But he says many times he's felt he was faking the "singer" part of his roles. No, honey, you can't fake that rich sound. (Getting a degree in music and playing in a symphony for nineteen years I've been around some amazing singers, so I think I make this assessment with some credibility.) Deb loves to hear Hugh sing. An early favorite of hers was the song "You and I" from *Chess*. And apparently she still asks him to sing it for her 20+ years later. Awwww.

After making music professionally for 20-ish years myself, the fun had gone out of it so I left that world behind. I played in a parent/teacher band for school fundraisers for a few years, which was a blast, and I picked up some improvisation skills. Now I play the piano for fun, help my daughter practice her violin, and mostly enjoy listening to others make music. Studying Hugh has reignited my love of musical theater, and I went to my first Broadway show last year, *Dear Evan Hansen*. As the mom of a teenage boy, I was holding back ugly-cry sobs by the end. What opens your soul that way?

Do I swoon over every note Hugh has ever sung? Not necessarily, but here are some of my top goosebump bringers:

- Hugh sang a gorgeous rendition of "Bethlehem Morning" at Carols By Candelight in 1997 in Melbourne. The last note is a glorious use of falsetto! I don't know why we don't hear that from him more often!

- A guaranteed pick-me-up for me is his version of "Oh What a Beautiful Morning." His voice is rich and powerful and joy radiates from him in waves. The first time I heard it was on a video of a British talk show while he was promoting *X-Men 2*. Answering questions about his early career in musical theater, he joked that his mates from drama school refused to pay to hear him sing. Of course the host asked him to sing a little, and when he started, my jaw literally dropped. That sent me immediately searching for the video of him in the full musical.

- Search for his "Have Yourself a Merry Little Christmas" from Saturday Night Live in 2001. I've only ever found an audio recording. Sure wish I could find video!

- Even though the 2002 Carnegie Hall performance of *Carousel* was a concert version, not staged, Hugh easily filled out the depth of the character in songs like "If I Loved You."

- It's a tough choice, but I think my favorite song from *The Boy from Oz* is "Come Save Me." I love hearing Hugh sing harmony, and I love the emotional power I can feel both from him and from his co-star, Stephanie Block.

- The duet with Aretha Franklin singing "Somewhere" at the 2005 Tony awards was sublime. His lower range makes my sternum vibrate.

- Sorry Josh Groban, but I prefer Hugh's version of "To Where You Are" by Richard Marx. This comment under the YouTube video of that performance makes me smile: "Omg when you think Hugh Jackman can't be any sexier…. And you find this video…"

- I've already mentioned that "From Now On" in the final workshop of *Showman* blew me away, but I think my favorite part of the soundtrack is when Hugh sings harmony on "A Million Dreams."

You see how I can gush about Hugh and music? What makes you gush like that? As Hugh said referring to the documentary *Bathtubs Over Broadway,* "The quirky thing that we love to do that everyone else thinks is ridiculous? It's a reminder to just keep doing it!" Getting regular doses of those things that light you up is more powerful than any vitamin.

Having said that, let's talk more about wellness…

CHAPTER 11

HUGH JACKMAN IS MY PERSONAL TRAINER

Find your best self-care.

Self-care is a key part of putting on your own oxygen mask first, but it's also really easy for self-care to become just one more thing you "should" do. So my most important message is to find what truly restores YOU.

For most of my adult life, health and wellness have been a series of red flashing SHOULDS in my head. I should eat vegan. I should eat Paleo. I should drink raw milk. Raw milk will kill you. Try the cereal diet. Cereal is the root of all evil. I should try jogging. My knees and lower back hurt when I jog. I should try swimming. Chlorine aggravates my asthma. I should...

Hugh didn't turn me into a bodybuilder, or even someone who enjoys exercise... at all. But he did help me love myself enough to settle down the chorus of *shoulds* and start to actually listen to MY body. And so far a couple habits I observed in him struck a chord in me that made them easy to incorporate: drinking more water and meditation. They are providing a new foundation of wellness based on true self-care.

For quite a few years, I had been decent at drinking water, but not great. As I watched more and more interviews with Hugh, I started noticing just how often he takes a drink while he's talking. I started taking screenshots of those moments and using them to inspire me to hydrate more. To turn it into a habit, for six weeks I tracked how many times a day I filled up my reusable water bottle, making sure it was at least three (it's a 27 oz bottle). Within a couple weeks, my body began to demand it. So now all I have to do is pay attention to how I feel and make sure I always have water nearby.

I had been vaguely thinking about meditating for a couple years. From everything I'd read and heard, it seemed like a useful practice, but different methods I tried didn't really stick. With Hugh and Deb's inspiration, I took the plunge to get trained in Transcendental Meditation, and it's been a life changer. Once again, I made checkmarks on a piece of paper for a few weeks to get myself in the twice-a-day habit, and now my body demands that as well. Occasionally I'll skip one of my sessions, but if I go more than 24 hours without it, I start feeling like my brain is running on EMPTY.

Meditation has been a daily habit for Hugh since his time at WAAPA, and he describes it very eloquently:

- To Oprah: "In meditation, I can let go of everything. I'm not Hugh Jackman. I'm not a dad. I'm not a husband. I'm just dipping into that powerful source that creates everything. I take a little bath in it."
- On *Good Morning America:* "If you can, twice a day, take the load off, drop all the masks, and be yourself, you end up living your life with a stronger, finer, clearer energy for everything you want to do. It somehow just seems to make life easier."
- In a documentary interview: "It's a different experience every time but I get glimpses of something that energizes me on such a deep level that now I'm not sure exactly what I'd do without that form of prayer. It's a way to be in touch with who I really am."

My description is a little less poetic. I say it's like "taking a shower for your brain." Or sometimes I explain it as my brain feeling like a clothes dryer with lots of thoughts tumbling around, and meditation is like stopping the dryer and folding the clothes, except I don't actually have to do anything. I just meditate and the clothes magically fold themselves.

In addition to twice daily meditation, another of Hugh's favorite types of self-care is weight training. He now loves the feeling of being strong so continues his routine even when it's not required for a role. Tap dancing is his favorite form of daily movement. Jigsaw puzzles are a favorite zen-like activity.

There are so many different kinds of self-care: hot baths, fancy coffee, vitamins, home-cooked meals, take-out food, manicures, walking the dog, even running errands by yourself can be self-care for a busy mom. Maybe it's a night out with girlfriends, maybe it's a night in a bookstore by yourself. The key thing is to try some things that intrigue you and find out what really refreshes you, what makes you feel really good. Hugh was asked how he defined luxury, and he said "It means treating yourself as important, in whatever form that takes." Yes, that!

I'm still on the journey of finding out what foods and what movement make my body feel really good. If you're searching with me, my friend Angela is currently writing a book called *The Diet Renegade*, about listening to your body's wisdom. Watch for it. But the bottom line is this: please, please, please, moms, and everyone, put on your own oxygen mask first.

One of the most important forms of self-care is positive self-talk. Be gentle with yourself. Notice what's going right. Know your priorities and know what's ok to let slide. And when you're depleted, rest. Ask for help. Hugh said, "I love my work, and if there's times when I'm tired, I will always back off." He doesn't ever want to feel like he doesn't have anything to give. He doesn't ever want to dread performing.

Persistent stress is linked to cancer, heart disease, and autoimmune disorders. On the other hand, happiness is proven to strengthen our immune systems and improve circulation. I agree with Hugh 100% that Joy is the real fountain of youth. When asked about aging, he said, "I feel I'm getting happier in my life. The older I am, the more I learn, and the more I can let go of the things that are exhausting in life."

Joy isn't a nice-to-have, it's a critical piece of your health.

CHAPTER 12

OLYMPIC-LEVEL MARRIAGE

Be all-in with your most important relationships.

You only have to listen to Hugh for about ten minutes to know where his priorities lie. "Our marriage is the foundation of our family and therefore my life." And, "Nothing I've accomplished as an actor or performer would mean very much to me without having a beautiful family to come back home to."

Hugh likes to use the phrase "Olympic-level," referring to Zac Efron's ability to slide shot glasses, or Australians' ability to party. And Hugh himself is talented in so many things (one-take axe throwing bullseye, just saying). But if there's one thing at which we know for sure he's Olympic-level, it's being a husband. It's swoon-worthy how he talks about Deb:

"...my secret weapon"
"...my rock"
"Underneath the surface, where it's real, where it's still, where it's deep, that is the love I have with Deb."

Hugh and Deb have an extraordinary marriage. In fact, at the risk of sounding melodramatic, studying their marriage and applying what I learned was a big factor in saving my own. They have the strongest relationship I've ever witnessed. Happily, we can learn from what they do and apply it ourselves! The first step is...

1. Choose someone who loves you just the way you are.

Hugh gave us a great lesson in choosing the right person in an interview with Marie Osmond. In response to her question about what makes a person attractive, he said:

> *Honesty is the greatest. When I say that I mean authenticity—when you meet someone and they are just confident and honest enough in themselves to be exactly who they are. And Deb had that in spades. In fact I don't think I'd ever met a woman like that. And instantly that makes you feel 'Well, I can just be me completely.' Even the bits that I don't normally show people, even the bits that are a little embarrassing or whatever.*

He told another interviewer he knew she was the one because, "I didn't have to be any other version of Hugh Jackman for her to love me." What a gift! What freedom! That level of unconditional love invites the authenticity that creates true intimacy.

He said it another way on Jeff Probst's show:

> *The incredible blessings I've had in my life, I know I wouldn't have had without her. Because when you meet that person who you match with, they get you to the core. You don't have to be anything, it's like the greatest relief in your life, you are just completely yourself. Flaws, good parts, everything. It's like being on the comfiest sofa you've ever been on, right? Every day of your life. And so you don't have to try and be anything. And that person, Deb for me, knows me 100%. She knew what I was capable of more than I knew. She encouraged me at times when I thought 'Oh, I don't know about that.'*

My own first marriage is a clear picture of the opposite. Remember that story about him telling me to lose 10 pounds before we took our engagement pictures? If I knew then what I know now... We were married five years, and it took quite a bit of counseling to put my self-esteem back together. Thankfully all those wounds have healed, and I now see him as someone who loved me as best he could at the time. (It took 12 years post-divorce for me to heal to that point, for the record, so if you're in that situation, give yourself some grace.)

Happily, the second time around I chose someone who loves me the way I am.

So how can you tell at the beginning of a relationship whether there's potential to be like Deb and Hugh? In an interview 20 years ago, Hugh gave us a good clue. He was asked about what he was like in his single days—what his approach to dating was. He said he loved learning about people. "I loved being seduced by a woman and seeing how they wanted to attract me, what it was like in their place, how they made love in their space, how they made breakfast in their place, what their place was like."

Whew, is it hot in here? There you have it. How **interested** is your date in the depths of who you are? How curious are they? How curious are you to know what makes them tick? What an excellent barometer.

2. **Maintain connection continually.**

Intimacy starts with accepting each other as you are, but it needs to intentionally be fed and kept alive, or you "grow apart," as many couples have experienced. I'm not sure Hugh and Deb even realize the power and the rarity of what they have created. I give Deborra-lee a lot of the credit for the foundation she established at the beginning to maintain intimacy. When asked about the secret to their successful marriage, they sometimes credit Deb's 'never apart for more than two weeks' rule. This makes most of us laugh. I'm rarely apart from my husband for two days! I don't think we've ever been apart for more than a week in the 17 years we've been married.

But the magic behind their rule is what Deb explains further, that without intentionally maintaining connection, people get used to making decisions or handling problems on their own, and they grow apart. What Hugh and Deb have done, probably better than any other couple, is to keep each other involved in the details of everyday life continually. Hugh says that when they're apart, they talk by phone more than 10 times a day. He Facetimed her from the Empire Awards in London during his acceptance speech for Best Actor (she was back in New York). Even when they are in the same city but going their separate ways during the day, they connect a lot. Just recently they were on Facetime while he was waiting for his entrance on *Live with Kelly and Ryan* and he kept her on as he came onto the set. She was just across town, but it had been a few hours since they'd talked. They keep each other included in their thoughts and decisions all day long.

This has been the secret sauce I started applying in my own marriage. It feels vulnerable to write, because only a few close friends were aware, but when I first started "studying" Hugh, my husband and I were on the verge of divorce. I was the one who wanted out. I was conflicted, because I knew Dave was (is) a really good man, but we just didn't feel connected, and I wanted more out of life than a roommate.

We decided to put everything we had into trying to make things good, so that if we did end up separating, we would know we'd done our best. A relationship coach was helping, but Hugh and Deb's example filled in a few important pieces. I found a new appreciation for how valuable it is to have a partner who wants me to be myself, who loves me just the way I am. We just needed to connect.

I was intrigued by Hugh and Deb's continual connection. It has been important to me since my ill-fated first marriage to be a strong, independent woman, to not be controlled by anyone. But observing their level of connectedness, I realized that getting your partner's input is very different from asking permission. Through their example, and through reading *The Queen's Code* by Alison Armstrong, I realized that when you work as partners, you can accomplish more. When you ask for and accept help, you can set higher goals and dream bigger dreams. I learned that talking about everyday details keeps you emotionally connected. I've consciously focused on sharing little details with my husband as we go through our day, letting him know any updates with the kids or in my work or activities. It's much easier for me to do that than try to download everything when he gets home from work, when we're both tired, everyone needs food, and the kids need to get to activities. We don't have to choose between taking time to catch up or growing apart, because we stay caught up throughout the day. Decisions I would have made on my own in the past, I now talk through with him, large and small. Not because I need his approval, but because it makes us more of a team. People say marriage "takes work." I don't use the word work because many people associate that with unpleasant tasks. Instead let's say it requires **focus** and **intention** to connect. Continually.

When you're used to making a lot of little decisions together, it's a lot easier to make the big decisions together. Hugh and Deb have talked about the agreement they made when they got married that at all turning points they would make decisions based on what was best for their family. That

doesn't seem revolutionary to me, it just seems like good sense. But maybe with two high-powered careers, being explicit about it is unique. And the magic is having the level of continual connection and mutual respect to carry it out.

Emotional connection makes physical connection so much better. And I can also admit that when I realized my husband's chest hair pattern was very similar to Hugh's, it, uh, helped. ☺

Which leads me to...

3. Be real about it ALL.

In addition to connecting in the details, intimacy is strengthened by being open and real throughout a life of changing and growing. That includes sharing the good, bad, and the ugly that you experience. Hugh says, "My wife is my lover, my best friend, and the first person I tell everything to, including the embarrassing, shameful, yucky stuff. Which is why we're still together." It was a huge "aha" for me to observe how Hugh and Deb are open about finding other people attractive. Because their connection is so deep, it's not threatened by their being human.

When asked about his favorite X-Men character, it's clear that Hugh is partial to one co-star. "My general rule is to do as many movies with Halle Berry as possible." Asked about which mutant Wolverine would marry, Jean Grey's name doesn't even come up. "I don't want to get in trouble with my wife, but maybe Storm." In another interview on the same question he gallantly says, "And I'm willing to fight any of you for it by the way."

A radio discussion of the Blurred Lines video led to him talking about reacting to other women and that Deb understands and says the same about other men. She thinks Brad Pitt is adorable, and when she did the TV show in Australia in 2016, she commented, "I wouldn't have minded if they'd thrown in a Hemsworth." And she readily admits to a long-time crush on Jerry Seinfeld.

A lot of us hide that kind of thing from our partner because we feel guilty, but it's part of being alive. As Hugh says, "It's crazy to kind of think that we're dead inside and are never going to look at anyone else." It's only a bad thing if you try to pretend it doesn't exist, because that can be the beginning of a wall between you and your spouse. A wall cuts off the flow of energy and connection, and causes you to start growing apart. It's all part of being awake, to feel all the feelings, then bring that energy into

your own relationship. At first, my husband was intimidated and a little worried about how intensely I was studying Hugh. But as he started reaping the benefits of my new level of aliveness, he embraced my new hobby. ☺

Of course #3 only works if #1 and #2 are already in place. When you have a deep connection with your partner, being real about your feelings isn't threatening. Here's one of the most intriguing aspects of Hugh's and Deb's relationship: while the longevity of their marriage is a rarity in Hollywood, I don't think they stay together out of moral obligation. They're together because their bond is so strong, they're so integral in each other's daily lives, that they can't imagine otherwise.

They stay together because of, wait for it, the JOY and the sanctuary they find in each other.

So while they're open about noticing others (let's be real, they're surrounded by some of the most genetically advantaged humans alive), there's never any doubt who comes first. When Katie Couric asked what leading lady he most wanted to work with the quick answer was, "My wife!" On a press tour in Asia Hugh said, "I was told I was going to be introduced by the most beautiful actress in the world and I presumed that was my wife."

The bottom line? "I love our wedding anniversary because it reminds me that everything is right in the world," Hugh said. Now that's a foundation.

4. Support each other's dreams

Deb and Hugh try not to work at the same time, so one can support the other. Again as a matter of practicality that doesn't work for most couples, but Dave and I are getting better at ensuring that we aren't both focused on big projects or goals at once.

In the interest of letting them be human, Hugh and Deb don't always manage a perfect balance. In July 2013 Hugh was talking about *The Wolverine* with David Letterman. Dave observed that Hugh had made several movies in a row, and Hugh said, "Has my wife been talking to you? Because this is a nightly conversation." He said he was invigorated by the work but was "pretty much in the doghouse at home." A few months later at a press conference in Zurich for *Prisoners*, a reporter asked what was next for him. After naming a couple possibilities, Hugh added, "Just in case

my wife is waking up in New York reading your publication, I am taking a break, Deborra-lee..."

Since Hugh is known for being a genuinely sweet person, interviewers often ask if he ever gets grumpy. Yes, when he gets overwhelmed because he's said yes to too many things. He credits Deb with gently pulling him back when he's getting over-committed.

It's an amazing feeling to know that your partner always has your back. Hugh again: "When you know that you're loved completely for who you are, no matter what comes and goes... when you know there's a rock there, that goes a long way, particularly in this business." I heard some echoes of his own experience when Hugh talked about P.T. Barnum's relationship with his wife in *The Greatest Showman.* Charity "loves her husband even though he doesn't fully love himself. She can see the whole man."

A key part of that support is helping you keep things in perspective. One of the sweetest stories I've heard Hugh tell is when they were filming the bullet train scene in *The Wolverine.* In one take of him getting flung out of the train and grabbing onto the outside, Hugh got a possible concussion and was sent home early. When he admitted what had happened, Deb's response was, "Use your stunt double! You're old! You are not Wolverine! You have children! Stop it!" Isn't that a sweet look into the dynamics of partners living the Hollywood life?

What's the equivalent in your world of your partner reminding you to use your stunt double?

5. Have FUN together!

Here's the rest of Hugh's answer to Marie Osmond about attraction.

> *Obviously there has to be a physical attraction, and my wife is probably one of the funniest people I've ever met, but she's open and positive and up, and through her – I've changed a lot with Deb. She's given me a lot of confidence, and she's just fun. Life is fun with her. And by the way, I was single when I met her, life was good – I was happy! And when I met her I was like 'Ok, there's my [single] life that I've created' [on one hand], and life with her was just 20 times better, it was a no brainer!*

It's easy for all of us to get bogged down in the details of running a household and raising kids, and we start to feel like roommates or business partners. Fun and romance don't have to be fancy, but they're important!

Hugh was asked in January of 2018 if he had a New Year's resolution or mantra for the year. A group of their friends had just made t-shirts that said "LLLDD" – Live Life Like Deb Does. "She has more fun than anybody I know," he said. I want an LLLDD shirt, don't you?

Hugh and Deb try to do weekly date nights. Trying new things together brings an automatic sense of adventure. "We pick a different 10-block radius and we'll go to Chinatown and have foot massages and find a new restaurant," Deb told *Vogue Australia*, "or go to the Upper East Side and go to Harlem." Connection is the key. "My husband is my best friend...I've always said, I was an only child so marriage to me is like a permanent sleepover with someone to play with in the morning, so I think it's awesome. I love it."

That doesn't mean a couple has to agree on everything! Hugh loves sports but Deb doesn't. Sometimes they each do their own thing, sometimes they compromise. "My wife and I are about to have our 22nd wedding anniversary, but our dining tastes differ a great deal. She likes a 45-minute affair; I like a long, drawn-out meal with wine pairings." They both agree on date nights at home drinking martinis and playing backgammon. And snowball fights. "We're very competitive," Deb says.

Hugh gets major points for romance. His secret? "Surprise." The key is breaking up normal routines and doing little unexpected things, like calling Deb and saying he'd been delayed on set and wouldn't be home until late, then showing up in the early afternoon to take her on an impromptu lunch date. So, gentlemen, when YOU plan a special outing or adventure, we women feel really spoiled. Just saying.

6. Express your appreciation

Hugh is Olympic-level at words of affirmation, too. He was asked about playing a tragic hero – someone with many burdens. Has he had hard times in life? Yes, "Prior to meeting my wife, many bumpy roads. Luckily when I met her, she infinitely made my life better in every way." Of course they've had hard times in their married life, too, but I certainly get the sense that the heavy stuff is much lighter because of the way they go through it together.

They celebrate each other. When Hugh got a Golden Globe nomination for *The Greatest Showman*, Deb had congratulatory banners up around the house when he got home. When Hugh was named Sexiest Man Alive in 2008, every interviewer wanted to know what Deb's reaction was. A wise woman, Deb's first response was, "I could have told them that years ago." Then just to keep him on his toes, she added, "Really? Brad Pitt didn't get it?" And she followed that up with, "Now take the garbage out, sexy boy." When reporters ask her what it's like being married to a sex symbol, her broad perspective is, "I hope every wife thinks she's married to the most charming man in the world."

For himself, Hugh keeps that particular honor in perspective. "I took that with a little smile. I know it was lobbied for by the studio at the time. Nothing but illusions! Believe me, I know who I am and what is real and what isn't."

While I admire his groundedness, there's no question Hugh can bring the heat. An interviewer asked him if he would ever get a tattoo, since some people have tattoos of him as Wolverine. He gave it some thought – would he consider a tattoo of a favorite sports team? No, he didn't want anything on his skin. Maybe a picture of his wife? No, no tattoos because "I can have her on my skin." Once again, is it hot in here?

And Hugh made all of us cry when he couldn't hold back tears paying tribute to Deb while accepting the Kirk Douglas Award for Excellence in Film, borrowing a few phrases from Mr. Rogers.

> *You have taught me that life is actually never defined by the highlight reel, life happens when the camera is not rolling. You've believed in me when I couldn't. You've loved me with a passion and a depth that I didn't even know existed, and I don't think I even felt that I deserved. You have pushed and encouraged me when I was scared to venture out.*
>
> *You have smiled me into smiling. You have sung me into singing. You have loved me into loving. And like everything I do in my life, I share this with you. I love you.*

The strongest relationship I've ever witnessed.

#1 and #2 are the foundation. Choose a partner with whom you can be your full self, and stay connected continually. The rest is gravy. (But don't underestimate gravy, it makes everything more delicious!)

I'm not saying all of this is easy to do! Asked about the biggest risk he has ever taken, the answer came instantaneously: "Marriage, the whole family life. It's not so much a risk as a surrender, kind of like, okay, I'm jumping into the rapids."

But the rewards are great. "What you learn being married to someone is better than any classroom or anything you can study, or any job," he said. "If I didn't have Deb, I don't know if I would've kept acting. With the risks, having someone's unconditional love means you can really fall on your ass and be completely loved, even if the rest of the world chucks tomatoes at you."

Deb's mom summed it up: "I'm blessed to have her as happy as she is. Hugh loves her as much as she loves him; they're beautiful together. I think that's all any mum wants—for her kids to be happy." I agree, Fay (may you rest in peace). That's what we all want.

CHAPTER 13

REVOLUTIONARY PARENTING

Let other people be who they are.

There's no quicker path to frustration than trying to control someone else's behavior. Ask any parent. So what's the Joy Revolution alternative?

> *I hope that my kids follow their passions, that they do what they want to do and not what anyone else tells them they should do. I want them to be authentic and true to themselves.*
> ~ Deborra-lee Furness

> *Everything is exposed with kids. There's no artifice, because they see you for exactly what you are.*
> ~ Hugh Jackman

How do you allow your kids to be who they are, encourage them to believe in themselves, and raise them to be kind, curious adults? One thing I know for sure is that kids absorb how we act far more than how we tell them to act.

One of the things I admire most about Hugh and Deb is we put a similar level of priority on our kids. Being a mom is my most important role right now, and the Jackmans seem to feel the same. Being fulfilled creatively and professionally is important, awards and fame come with the territory, but Hugh said, "the most pressing thing for Deb and me now? Helping the kids reach their potential. And having fun."

While the kids were young it worked best in their family for Deb's primary job to be parenting while Hugh was the primary breadwinner, but they're both very involved. Hugh was the chief bedtime-story-reader, and often made up stories at the kids' request. There's a very sweet video of the family taking a hot air balloon ride when Oscar was about four, and as they took off, Hugh can be seen massaging Oscar's ears to help with the pressure change.

When each child was born, Deb got a book engraved "From Dad" and Hugh writes in it once a week or so, memories and stories of their lives. He plans to give them to the kids when they each turn 21. Isn't that a beautiful idea? Once when Hugh's luggage got lost on a flight, he was pretty chill about it until he realized those journals were in the suitcase. Thankfully it was found.

Hugh and Deb have talked about navigating parenting when you have different parenting styles. Hugh said in *Good Housekeeping* that their parenting habits were different since he was one of five kids with a very straight-laced father, while Deb was the only child of a single mother. "We're drifting closer together, but it's a constant negotiation. She loosens me up, and I give her a little more structure." I'll be honest right up front, my parenting style more closely aligns with Deb's.

Hugh jokes that he read a lot of parenting books, but apparently his kids didn't read any of them, because it didn't match. I think that means Hugh was reading the wrong books. ☺ Because my favorite parenting books really fit with my instincts, which matched what my kids seemed to need. *Siblings Without Rivalry* and other books by Adele Faber and Elaine Mazlish were favorites. I love that Deb was involved in the launch of the book *Out of Control: Why Disciplining Your Child Doesn't Work* by Dr. Shefali Tabary. I completely agree that kids don't need to be controlled, they need support in learning to understand their emotions. They need mentoring while they practice making decisions. The previous chapter about marriage was mostly learning from what Hugh and Deb have done. This parenting chapter will be mostly what has worked for me.

Ever since I started learning about our autopilot brain, and that the messages we hear as kids are a big part of how it gets programmed, my focus has been to raise kids who have positive programming and who follow their inner guidance instead of external rules.

In my journey to raise Joy Revolutionaries, the first thing I learned is what doesn't work.

When I caught myself whining at my daughter, "Why can't you be more positive??" I had to stop in my tracks and laugh at myself. Not only was it counterproductive, it was just plain ridiculous. When I realized that raising joyful kids had more to do with examining my own emotions before I interacted with them, things really smoothed out.

The first step is always being really aware of YOUR thoughts about your kids. So when I would catch myself thinking something like "my daughter's room is always a mess," or "I don't know if they'll ever become more responsible about their homework," I would stop and say, Wait. That is NOT where I want my autopilot steering. Time for a different approach.

Now when I have those moments, I stop and make a mental list of all the ways my kids are amazing. They're unbelievably focused when they're doing the things they love. The more freedom I give them, the more responsible they become. *When I see them as their best selves*, the words that come out of my mouth, and my tone of voice, are completely different.

This has played out in an almost comical way in the past in how the kids sometimes reacted differently to me and to my husband based on our expectation. My husband used to comment that the kids didn't listen to him the way they listened to me, and of course the difference was not really in the kids. The kids were the same, he and I were the variables. The two of us said things differently. I have gotten pretty good at going into any interaction with them expecting a good outcome. If I'm asking them to fold their clean clothes or to unload the dishwasher, I know it will get done. Sometimes I have to go back and remind them, but then I know it's because they were really engrossed in what they were doing, so my reminders come out gently. The bottom line is, the most important thing to me is that my kids and I are always on the same side. We have the same goals, of having a peaceful, cooperative household, and of them becoming happy, healthy adults.

It bears repeating – when I see them as their best selves, the energy I bring to our interactions enables them to show up that way.

The "flip the but" trick in Chapter 2 is especially important in how you talk to your kids. Compare these two statements:

I love you, but your messy room is driving me crazy!

I know I comment on the clothes on the floor of your room a lot, but I also want to remind you that I love you, and you have so many strengths.

One starts with connection then erases it. The other creates connection. It's the same content, but flipping which one came before the "but" makes a striking difference. Whatever comes before the but is minimized, so put the "bad" stuff there, and the good stuff after.

I've learned that when I am worried about my kids' ability to do something, they can feel that in my body language, my tone of voice, and how my words come out. Of course that affects their confidence. I'm getting better at catching my own train of thought before it picks up momentum. If I'm concerned about their inability to get a project done, nagging them only reinforces in their brain that they're not capable of completing it. Instead, I might ask what their plan is and if they want any help from me keeping focused. I'm happy to give reminders, but I always want them to feel *we're in it together*.

Does anyone else worry about what their kids eat? That's obviously a rhetorical question. What I most want is for my kids to listen to their own bodies, and eat what makes them feel healthy and strong. That means I have to let it go and trust them. Because we're partners, I remind them to listen to their bodies – to stay hydrated, or to balance sugar with protein.

A common area of struggle in a lot of households is screen time. Again, what I want most is for my kids to listen to their bodies and know what their brains can and can't handle. I use the "look into their eyes" test. When one of them has been playing a game or watching a video for a period of time, I have them look at me. If their eyes have a vacant look, I remind them it's time to take a break and walk around, look out the window, bounce a ball, pet the dog, talk to me, whatever works. It's been very cool to see them adopt that awareness for themselves.

Did I mention that we don't do punishment and don't have a lot of rules? When you understand how the human brain works, you understand how counterproductive punishment is. It actually strengthens the autopilot leading kids toward the unwanted behavior.

Ok, we have had a *few* rules in our house. But truly a very few.

You have to hold my hand in a parking lot (as a toddler).
You have to wear your seatbelt.
You have to brush your teeth.

Truly, I think that's it. And now that they're teenagers, I don't have to enforce any of those anymore. They do it on their own.

We do, however, have a LOT of **agreements**.

We agree on a bedtime that allows them to be healthy and function at school. The kids' main responsibility in the family is to get educated. When we got them phones, we discussed that it was a milestone indicating they had reached an age of responsibility – that along with their phones comes the responsibility for how they spend their time. They use their phones for wake-up alarms, time-to-leave-for-school alarms, and homework reminders. They also agree to unload the dishwasher when it's clean, in exchange for their allowance. They fold their own clean clothes in exchange for YouTube Premium (which is really a win for me since I like that they don't see ads!) When we have issues (because we're all human), we never threaten to take things away, just simply remind them of what we've agreed.

One more time, when you see your kids as their best selves, it makes it easier for them to show up that way!

My goal all along has been to raise kids who have a strong inner compass instead of doing things because I say so. I try not to react negatively to anything they tell me, because I know their solution would be to simply stop telling me things. And nothing is more important to me than my kids knowing they are safe telling me anything, that we can work through anything together.

That's another reason we've never done punishment. It reinforces bad behavior and only results in them finding ways not to get caught. But from a very young age, we didn't shield them from natural consequences. When they got teeth and would bite down while nursing (normal behavior, but not something I was going to live with), I would say, "Ouch! I will never hurt your body, and you may not hurt my body." I'd put them down for a few seconds then say, "Would you like to try again?" Of course a nine-month-old baby wasn't comprehending my words, but I wanted to be consistent with that standard (we don't hurt each other) from the very beginning. On the few occasions when one of my kids lashed out physically at the other, I completely ignored the perpetrator and went overboard soothing and loving on the "injured" party. It was a natural consequence that diffused the situation, then we would regroup and go about our day.

At the risk of being redundant, my most important intention in parenting is for them to always know we're on the same side. We all intend for them to grow up happy, healthy, and good at making decisions. We all want to enjoy life! I have always tried to say yes to their requests unless there's a good reason to say no, which has made them generally respect my judgement. I model putting on my own oxygen mask first, because sometimes the reason for a no is that I'm too tired or can't fit it into my schedule. If it's a financial decision, sometimes my answer is "We don't have the money for that right now but let's think about where it might come from," or "It doesn't feel to me like that's where we want to spend our money right now." Decisions are usually open to discussion – they're always welcome to try to convince me to see something their way, in fact sometimes I specifically ask them to build a detailed case for what they want or research a plan and come back to me.

So what do you do if you're in a negative pattern with your kids?

You don't have to change your kid. Seriously. When you change your programming, you will bring out a completely different side of them. That's the good news—as *you* shift, the pattern will change quickly! Kids' brains are much more pliable than ours.

Your most important mind work is going to be done when you're not with them—either when they're at school or sleeping, not in a moment of conflict. Take out a notebook and pen and write down all the best characteristics of your kids. As you write, be aware of your emotional state, and watch for a shift in how you feel—that's how you know your autopilot is changing.

Do this several days in a row, several times a day if you can. If you need more to write, write out your happiest memories with them, or write out scenarios of how you wish your interactions would go. Handwriting is a shortcut to reprogramming your autopilot brain.

Then when you're with your kids again, preemptively focus on the best things about them. When something unwanted happens, take some deep breaths, step back and notice your emotion before you act or react. If your emotion is "I have to fix this unwanted behavior" then don't act, because you'll actually reinforce the pattern. Repeat under your breath the best things about your kid until you can feel your emotion shift, then talk to them.

Before I had kids, I thought it would be my job to "mold" them into good adults. But now I realize they were already wise little beings, and really we are on an adventure together to help each other become the fullest versions of ourselves.

I'm certainly not saying every day is perfect. But our primary focus is on a relationship of trust and connection. When I see them as their best selves, I bring out the best in them. And that makes every situation easier!

CHAPTER 14

DO WHAT YOU LOVE. REALLY.

Trust Joy. Even in business.

People have asked Hugh, "How do you become a star?"

His answer? "I have absolutely no idea." What he does know is that he was "the happiest I'd ever been at that point in my life" at drama school. That's my answer—you do what you love.

Success stories usually talk about hard work and persistence and determination. The mystery is, where do those characteristics come from? What makes some people so motivated? Can it be taught?

There are three things that motivate us as humans: carrots, sticks, and joy. Sticks (rules, requirements, and fear of punishment) are the least effective. They might bring about a short term increase in motivation, but that quickly is lost, and in the long term they wear you down and stifle motivation. Carrots (incentives, rewards, and paychecks) can be very effective to help you focus, but if they don't match your own long-term goals or if the incentive isn't something you enjoy, the motivational effect can wear off. The absolute strongest and most sustainable source of motivation is what comes from inside you. A dream or an idea you have, or finding an area where you can really excel and make a difference in the world, leads to wild success.

Here's what you can learn from Hugh to apply the Joy Revolution to your career.

1. Do what sounds fun, even when it doesn't appear to be practical.

Hugh's career is a testament to the power of doing what attracts you, what excites you. There were several times after Hugh graduated from college that people could have told him he "should" get a real job. He had completed a degree in journalism, but was feeling the pull toward acting. So instead of looking for a permanent job, he kept working part time at the gym and decided to take an acting class. How many parents or career coaches would have questioned his choice? Then he was offered a good-paying role on a soap opera, but decided to turn it down to get more acting training. Aren't we glad Hugh's dad supported him following his dreams?

Hugh is confident that when you follow your gut, the future will take care of itself. During his time on Broadway in *The Boy from Oz*, an interviewer asked, "You're not worried about your film career losing momentum?" Hugh simply said, "No, I don't worry about those kinds of things." In fact, several people had advised him not to take the role, but he said "it just felt right." (His two most important advisors—Deb and Patrick—were all for it, for the record.)

There was even that ONE time when Hugh's instincts were different from Deb's, but he followed his gut anyway, going ahead with the audition for *X-Men*. Smart move, Hugh.

Even your closest, most trusted advisors don't know better than your OWN heart.

About ten years into his acting career, some well-intentioned mentors told Hugh his range was too wide – that there was too much variety in the projects he chose so directors didn't know what his specialty was. They said he needed to focus on one area. But that didn't sound fun to him, so he kept doing whatever he was drawn to. He loves being able to sing and tap dance on stage, then push the limits of his dramatic ability on the next project. So he ignored those voices. And now pretty much everyone (including some of those same people) sings his praises for being the guy who can do a little bit of everything.

So is it best to focus on one thing and get really good at it, or do a variety of things? I'm hoping by now the answer comes to you before I say it. **Whichever you want.** *Do you like going as deeply as you can into one singular focus, or do you like mixing it up? What you like tells you where your strengths are.*

Following your dreams doesn't have to mean drastic changes. Hugh realized there were connections between the journalism training he'd gotten and his dreams of acting. "I was very idealistic as a student. I pictured myself as a radio stringer somewhere in the Middle East, filing reports, changing the world, all that sort of thing. But I realized I didn't have the passion or the skill or the personality for it. But then I realized that the journalist's job—the love of stories and the quest to understand human nature and report back—was part of an actor's job too."

And now, in 2019, Hugh is on a world tour. Why? As he told *Billboard*, "It feels like if you're into golf and you get to play the best golf courses in the world the whole summer. It's a complete indulgence." This is how much he believes in doing what you love: "I have a rule—if I hear the intro to a song and don't get a tingle, then I take it out [of the set list]. For me it has to feel like, 'I can't wait to sing this song.'" Of course we expect many more intriguing movie roles in Hugh's future, but the stage is his favorite. "If it's not arenas, that's okay. But if you told me I'd never get to perform live again, I'd be pretty upset."

What do you do that makes time melt away and you lose track of the outside world because you are so in your zone? What energizes you? Look for ways you can incorporate more of those things into your career. When you find what lights you up, you will naturally go all in for what you want.

2. Try different things. Sometimes you find gold where you least expect it.

Playing a superhero with claws wasn't the way Hugh imagined his big break. He had no idea who Wolverine was. He had heard of a local rock band in Sydney called The Uncanny X-Men but had no idea they got their name from a comic book. And Deb certainly didn't think Hugh's talent would be best utilized playing a hairy mutant. (To reiterate, it's the ONLY time Deb has ever been wrong, and the ONLY time Hugh ever ignored her advice.) But it turned out to be the door that gave him the freedom to do everything else. "It has really been the spine of my career. It has allowed me to do a lot of other things. Fans have loved it. I've really loved playing him. And it has been the biggest surprise of my career."

For me, my direct sales business has played a similar role. I didn't think this business model worked for normal people, I thought it was only for highly extroverted, obnoxiously pushy people. (And honestly, companies who encourage their reps to be inauthentic give our industry a bad name.) But it checks the boxes of a lot of things I'm passionate about, like being kind to our planet and being good to our bodies. And while a lot of green and healthy things seem to be more work, I found one that is actually easier! The best part is that building a team reignited my interest, from my corporate training days, in the science of human performance and motivation. Now the bulk of my time is spent helping other women believe in themselves, which is pretty much my dream job.

3. Motivation flows when you're in the right career and you believe in yourself.

Leaders who share adages like 'Dreams don't work unless you do' misunderstand how our brains work. If you have to shame someone into working hard, they're not in the right career, or something has squelched their motivation and their Belief Engines need to be reset. Sure, it's possible to find success by forcing yourself to slog through things you find unpleasant. But it's certainly not the quickest way, because you're not using your whole brain.

Hugh is often referred to as the hardest working actor in show business. But the funny thing is, no one ever referred to him as the hardest working journalism student. He readily admits to doing the minimum needed to get by while working on that degree. Now, "I don't feel like I've worked a day in my life," he reflects. "My dad was an accountant and I know this might sound funny, but he absolutely loved it. I always try and encourage my kids to do things they love, no matter what they are."

Hugh goes all-in with everything he chooses to do, from researching a role to physical workouts. He might even go a little too far. Joining the 1000-pound club is an amazing achievement. But singing *Oklahoma!* with a migraine so bad you're throwing up between scenes? That's what understudies are for, dude. And then there's the time he had pneumonia and tried to sing anyway but had to ask his understudy to take over part way through the performance. (Maureen Lipman loves to tell that story since she stayed on stage and chatted with the audience while they made the switch.) Hugh's understudy in *The Boy from Oz* bemoaned that he never once got to go on, even when Hugh had stress fractures in his feet and was icing them four times a day to get through performances. Maybe since Hugh has never been anyone's understudy, he doesn't understand how much they look forward to getting the call!

But I love that what drives him is a love for what he does, not external forces. He told a group of entrepreneurs, "I understand people might say 'Oh, well, you've made it, you're successful now,' but for many years I wasn't. But all along, I loved it. I would put in 15 or 16 hours a day every day because I loved it! I never missed a day of drama school."

Deb also emphasizes the importance of doing what you're passionate about, referring to her work as a humanitarian. "I think passion counts for so much, sometimes even over expertise and skill. If you have a passion, necessity is the mother of invention, you want to get to that end goal. Your passion can drive you, and you do get creative along the way. That's what I had to do. I had no experience with boards, I had no experience with organizations, social media..." She emphasizes knowing your strengths, and surrounding yourself with people who are good at the pieces you need.

"Find the thing you're good at, the thing that you love, and do it for other people, and you're going to be on the right track." That's Hugh's career advice. "I believe talents are given for a reason. That's why you're here. That's why you're drawn to it."

Follow your bliss. Trust joy.

If you haven't yet found that sweet spot, how do you move toward it? Here's what Hugh says: "Write down five things you love to do. Next, write down five things that you're really good at. Then just try to match them up! Revisit your list once a year to make sure you're on the right track."

4. Dreaming big is key in any career.

Hugh's whole professional adventure has been fueled by dreams. He reflected in 2018, "We invest so much time into, you know, we go to the gym, we work out, all these things, and what I've learned over the years is to invest time in really believing, concentrating, and dreaming as big as you can go. It will come true. It will. It's incredible." Go back to Chapter 2 if you want to review the brain science of how dreaming makes things happen.

Remember that photo of himself in front of the Cottesloe (now known as the Dorfman) Theatre, part of the Royal National Theatre, when he was 21? That was a dream, even though he still wasn't sure he could make a living as an actor. That dream played a role in his decision to turn down the offer from *Neighbors* to pursue more acting training.

Follow your gut and don't sell yourself short! #whatwouldHughdo

During an interview in Berlin when *The Greatest Showman* was released there, he was asked what dreams still "keep him awake."

> *For me, for my career, for the world, I want to build and create. I believe that you've got to have the imagination – visualize it then go out and create it.*

And no, your dreams don't need a deadline.

I really cheered when I heard Hugh answer a question about goals. He said he wasn't a big believer in goals because what if what's possible is bigger than you can imagine? YES! YES! YES! The only time I've heard him mention a specific goal was, "My goal was to pay my rent as an actor." That's a good starting point for adulting, but magic happens when your dreams grow bigger. He said in 2010, "I try to avoid specific goals because at the end of the day I find those kind of goals limiting. Pretty much everything that has happened to me in the last 10 years I wouldn't have thought about 15 years ago." If Hugh had set specific goals and stuck to a pre-determined plan instead of following what he enjoyed, he'd probably be a successful TV interviewer instead of an international superstar. Not that it would have been a bad career, but oh boy, how the world would have missed out.

I hope this goes without saying, but to be clear, dreaming is for all ages. At age 58 Deb said, "My dream when I grow up is to direct a full-length picture." Now that the kids are getting older and more independent, she's working on that as I write.

Having said all that, the most important thing regarding goals is to trust how it FEELS to you. If you get a thrill out of setting a specific goal and smashing it, keep doing that! When setting a timeline creates more angst than excitement, don't do it, because it's giving fuel to a non-Belief Engine. Abraham Hicks says as long as it feels positive, keep getting more specific with your dreams. If it feels anxious, be more general, maybe even letting go of the outcome entirely. When you get good at paying attention to your emotional guidance, you'll know when to set specific goals, and when to go with the flow.

5. Start small and do what you do very well.

Dream big but start small and focus on doing things well. I know it doesn't seem like Hugh started small, landing lead roles on stage and screen right out of school, but he took the time to really learn in each role. He took singing lessons and spent time watching the other actors sing during *Beauty and the Beast*. And the smaller TV roles he had in between stage productions helped him hone his skills on the screen. Obviously that focus paid off. Director James Mangold said, "He's like a fine musical instrument. He can play comedy and go light, but he's also capable of delivering a performance of tremendous power. He's got this incredible masculinity and strength, and the courage to throw that all away and do a musical on Broadway."

The start of Laughing Man Coffee is another great example. David Steingard, co-founder, said, "There was very little business plan. What was interesting about this, and what I think has seeped into the culture [of the business], is this was all very organic. We had zero idea what was going to happen. Our first reaction was, let's open a café, buy coffee from Dukale in Ethiopia, tell his story, and sell it." They watched which parts were being most successful and perfected those further, and opportunities to grow started coming their way. The café itself never had a marketing budget, it was all word of mouth. And that led to the opportunity for global distribution, which was a no-brainer because it drastically increased the potential impact of Laughing Man Foundation.

A bedrock of Laughing Man Coffee is something Hugh learned from his father, the Price Waterhouse accountant. "Good business is good for everyone. If it's not good for everyone, it's not good business."

6. Focus on YOUR dreams, not the competition

David says of Laughing Man, "People always ask who's our competition. I've never looked at it that way. Our competition is ourself. We set out to do this thing." He expands that advice to everyone.

> *As an entrepreneur, you're surrounded in the news by the ultimate success stories. You have to stay centered and balanced in yourself. Don't worry about other people. Don't compare yourself to anybody. Be aware of what's going on, take it in, but don't judge yourself or criticize yourself based on what anybody else is doing. Know your trajectory, know where you have to get to, and find a way to keep that balance. Because as soon as you start playing the comparison game, you will never feel like you have enough physical resources and internal resources to meet the challenges you face.*

There's nothing I can add to improve that advice. So good.

7. Things come and go, and it's good to follow that, too.

Hugh also followed his gut about when it was time to say goodbye to Wolverine. Though fans still clamor daily on social media for him to come back, he's loving his post-superhero life. *The Greatest Showman* became a sensational fan hit, with a culture-changing, multi-platinum, record-breaking soundtrack. It earned him a Grammy, leaving him just an Oscar away from the joining the extremely rare EGOT club. I have confidence that will come.

And he still feels like part of the superhero family. "I feel I'm still at the dinner table, but I'm just not cooking and cleaning up anymore. It's nice. It's time for someone else to go and do the heavy lifting. Literally heavy lifting."

When I first got serious about making the Joy Revolution into a book (maybe even a series of books and workshops), I thought I had to choose between working on my business and writing the book. Now I get that they're the same path. Researching and writing has honed my skills as a leader in a way I never imagined. I have slowed the growth of my business because there are so many other fun things going on, but I'm enjoying leading my team more than ever.

And speaking of fun things...

CHAPTER 15

SEXIEST GOOFBALL ALIVE

Laughter really is the best medicine.

I love Hugh's sense of humor. I've watched thousands of hours of interviews he's done, and many times I find myself laughing out loud, or at least having a big cheesy grin on my face! When taking the photo of all the 2013 Academy Award nominees, Hugh was standing right next to the Oscar statue. "My inner seven-year-old wanted so badly to give the statue bunny ears..."

One of my favorites that never fails to cheer me up (yes, I've watched it probably forty times) is during *Eddie the Eagle* publicity when he *pretends* to drink a bottle of gin on camera, to play a joke on Taron. I'm guessing the gag was the reporter's idea, but Hugh plays his part SO WELL, Taron is completely sucked in, even knowing what a "bloody Thespian" Hugh can be. If you've never seen that interview, do yourself a favor and search for it on YouTube right now.

Another of my favorite moments is during his second time on *Inside the Actors Studio*, talking about *Les Mis*. He was asked about working with Colm Wilkinson, the original Broadway Jean Valjean, who plays the bishop in the movie musical version. Hugh noted that in the original concept album, Valjean was a deep baritone voice, but Colm changed it into the virtuoso tenor role it is now. While they were filming the scene where Valjean steals silver from the bishop, Wilkinson commented the last note of his part was too low. With a huge grin, Hugh said, "Suck it, Colm!"

So many times he's been asked by reporters about when Wolverine the Musical is coming. Usually when he gets asked that question, he says it's

Fox's worst nightmare. But backstage at the 2012 Tony Awards he was feeling cheeky, and his answer was, "Oh yeah, that's coming. I've been working on it for a long time it's just a lot of people don't see the vision. I don't know why."

I'm sure getting asked the same questions over and over again, he has to liven things up sometimes just to keep it interesting for himself. Since he's told stories of Deb asking him to wear costumes home at night, he's been asked many times if that includes Wolverine, claws and all. "Absolutely! The sheets we go through..." he joked.

Few people can match Hugh's deadpan ability. Sometimes I wonder if reporters whose native language isn't English catch his dry humor, like in an interview for Croatian television when he talked with a perfectly straight face about swapping partners during the filming of *Australia.* He regularly sends his publicist over the edge; when an interviewer tries to get him to take his shirt off he usually responds with an "I will if you will" deal.

But the greatest power of a healthy sense of humor is being able to laugh at yourself. After the scary stunt-gone-wrong on *Oprah* in Australia, Hugh was game to spoof himself by being shot out of a cannon (well, having a look-alike dummy shot out of a cannon) on the *Jonathan Ross Show*, while promoting *Real Steel*. A few years later, while promoting *Eddie the Eagle*, he was a great sport about Jonathan's game, "Hugh Jackman or Sweet Potato?" Google it. ☺

We all have those moments in life that pop into our mind over and over and make us cringe. I learned from Hugh that you take the power out of those moments by embracing them. Own it, make it part of your story, like the story of Hugh's "most embarrassing moment" on stage. If you want to hear it directly from him (and it's worth it), he's told the story several different times. The most detailed version was on *Enough Rope* in April 2004, so search for that. But here's the gist.

During *Beauty and the Beast,* Hugh's first professional stage show, he started getting chronic headaches. A naturopath quickly figured out he was dehydrated from the extra workouts and singing and dancing every night, so told him to drink about two liters of water a day. Hugh is an overachiever so drank about twice that amount the following day.

He went to the bathroom just before going onstage, but since he was so well hydrated it wasn't long before he had to go again. Gaston is a pretty physical role – carrying Belle around and dancing while singing. And he quickly figured out the muscles that are used to hold in urine are the same muscles you have to release to sing! He got to the end of the song "Me," which ends on a long high note, and it was decision time – to stay clenched and not sing it, or to let go and, well, let go! Our showman figured the performance mattered most, so out came the sound, and everything else!

Hugh sums it up, "I have to say that is the most humiliating moment, but funnily enough I don't mind retelling it. So what does that tell you?" It tells us you are a mature, open, confident person who has learned the freedom and joy in being human and fully living, and we love you for it.

He also freely shares the story of all the wolf research he did between being cast in *X-Men* and when he started shooting. Not only had he not read any of the comic books, he didn't know a wolverine was a real animal. Excellent intention to be well prepared, but he missed a few key details!

Hugh admires that quality when he sees it in others, too. "I think, to be honest, one of the greatest things I ever heard was when Halle Berry turned up for the first time ever to accept her Razzie Award for Catwoman. She said, 'Hey. If you're going to turn up and put on a dress to accept an Oscar, then you've got to be prepared to turn up and accept this one.' And I feel like—you know what? That is probably the coolest, most wise thing I've ever heard in this business."

Many, many interviewers ask Hugh, "You sing, you dance, you act; is there anything you can't do?" And he gives the same answer every time. "I'm a terrible handyman." Probably a lot of wives wish their husbands would admit that and hire professionals instead of trying things themselves! He also has said he's not a good driver; that his car growing up was nicknamed the "golf ball" because it had so many dings in it. Here's hoping he has improved in that area since having children!

For as graceful as he is either dancing or fighting, Hugh says, "It's kind of amazing to me that I can ever look vaguely sort of action-y or cool because I am clumsy." He was referring to the blooper of him trying to cut through a sail during the filming of *Pan*. It's a very ominous scene, where we see Blackbeard's silhouette slowly advancing with a sword drawn. But after several huge whacks, Hugh wasn't even able to poke a hole in the cloth! He recalled a crew member yelling, "Come on Wolverine! Get it together!" He says every film has a gag reel of him "tripping over, falling over, running into doors, knocking people over, punching myself with claws…"

At the Santa Barbara International Film Festival, Hugh found himself at the same table as Bo Derek, the object of his ski-jumping-is-like-an-orgasm scene in *Eddie the Eagle.* While accepting his award that night, He gleefully poked fun at himself. "I never thought for a second I would be sitting next to my wife, opposite a table from The Bo Derek, talking about fictitiously making out. There's some fantasy in there I think I've crossed off the list."

Life is supposed to be fun! And the more comfortable you are in your own skin, the more comfortable others are being around you.

CHAPTER 16

UPLIFTER IN CHIEF

When you're lit up inside, you naturally uplift others.

If the Joy Revolution is being clear on what you want and how you feel, how does that harmonize with being considerate of others?

There's a very important distinction between living your life to please others, and being so lit up that you can't help but uplift others. Even the word "considerate" offers some good clues. It's good to "consider" how your actions will affect others, but that's very different from automatically defaulting to what others want. I can consider your feelings without placing that as a higher priority than being true to myself. It comes back to putting on your own oxygen mask first. If you abandon yourself to defer to the needs of others, you have nothing to give.

But when you're lit up, you can't help but light up those around you.

When your tank is full and you have joy overflowing, it's easy to put yourself in other people's shoes to connect with them. For instance, how does Hugh find freshness performing eight times a week on stage? He said he loves to stand just off stage to hear the buzz of the audience right before the house lights go down. He uses that moment to remember that while it may be his 237th performance of the same material, it is the highlight of someone's year, maybe even a once-in-a-lifetime experience. With that awareness, he can connect with the audience with an open heart, and together they create something that's different every night.

What astounds me is how Hugh seems to bring the same intention to interactions with people in everyday life. It's important to him to ask

187

someone's name, whether it's the waiter in a restaurant or the sound guy at a press conference, and he remembers them! (That's why Deb calls him Senator Jackman.) When someone uses my name, it's an instant reminder that they really see me, and they're talking directly to me. I'm getting better at following Hugh's example of looking people in the eye and really focusing on them when I'm interacting, even if it's very brief.

Hugh's mum was a firm believer that every person on the planet, in every job or role, needs to feel appreciated, and she drummed that into her kids. That combined with Hugh's natural charisma is quite a vibration-raising force.

I'm guessing pretty much every person Hugh interacts with feels better about themselves afterward. That's a very special skill that I appreciate all the more because it's one of my life goals. When people ask Hugh how he's such a nice guy, he often credits being brought up to have good manners. But how Hugh uplifts others goes way beyond politeness. In fact, on set they call it "the Jackman effect." Everyone shows up at a higher level when he's around, not out of guilt or competition, but because they're inspired!

During their experiment with producing, Hugh didn't really enjoy the details of the work, the part he loved was finding new talent. "I love that feeling of enabling people to do what they do well." I think he has now discovered he can do that all day every day, from any position, just by being himself. He doesn't have to be in the role of a producer to accomplish that.

Hugh's co-stars rave about their experience. One of the most fun relationships to observe is with Keala Settle. The way Hugh has encouraged Keala in her journey to movie stardom is heart-melting. He calls her one of "the most talented, authentic, real, generous" people he's ever met. Keala struggled with stage fright, and at one point she left acting and became a stagehand for three years. The world didn't really see the full power of her talent until the final workshop to get *Showman* greenlit. Hugh, along with director Michael Gracey, convinced her to sing the role of Lettie in the workshop, and the rest is history. Plus, Hugh's impact on Keala hasn't just been work-related. He helped her through her mother's death in 2016, and when she had a mini-stroke in 2018, Hugh and Deb talked to her every day through her brain surgery and several months of recovery.

Even when the spotlight is on him, Hugh makes sure others feel appreciated. When Marie Osmond was interviewing him, he interjected, "Can I just say something before we move on? Your voice is ridiculous.

Your talent is amazing. You are a true artist." He and Deb had gone to see Donny & Marie: Christmas in Los Angeles a couple months before. And I've lost count of the number of times he makes a point of complimenting interviewers on their choice of questions or on their research.

The way he compliments people is poetic, but it's genuine. And it has an almost magical effect, because when you see someone as their best self, you bring it out in them.

His relationship with his mother reflects his ability to see the best in people. While her leaving was incredibly painful for Hugh, he said as he got older he realized, "Mum and Dad did their best with what they had." I admire Hugh's awareness that holding on to resentment doesn't help anyone. I admire his ability to open his heart to his mom.

He has also said his mom is his "toughest critic." *Here come my strong opinions on parenting again, but if there's any role that's not productive for a mom to play, it's toughest critic. There are enough critics in the world. The good news is, if anyone is reading this and starting to feel you've been too critical of others in the past, the way forward is to start by being gentle with yourself, because being critical comes from our own low self-esteem. I didn't believe that at first, I always thought I was easier on others than on myself. But when I started loving myself more, suddenly I felt differently toward others and found it much easier to see the best in them.*

Here's another secret. It's easier to genuinely acknowledge others when you are able to gracefully accept compliments yourself. When Hugh learned that Nicole Kidman said about him, "Isn't he the most popular man in the world?" his response was "I'm going to blush, that's a very, very sweet compliment." Isn't that a gracious reply? Another interviewer asked him to sum up his own best quality in one word. "Courage," he said. *Yes! It takes practice to authentically answer that question, but being able to articulate your strengths is such an important piece of good mental health. When I'm coaching people who have a habit of negative self-talk (which is most people, honestly, especially women), I start by asking them to write down three things they most admire in themselves. Can you do it?*

It's good that he can accept it, because the way other people talk about him is sometimes breathtaking. I have to share a few of my favorites. These reflect what it's like to work with a person who is truly lit up from the inside.

"There's this really positive, generous energy about him. He meditates every day, and he's not out for himself. He wants to lift other people up. And really humble as well."
~ Rachael Beck, co-star in *Beauty and the Beast*

"He comes out and he has the audience in the palm of his hand. Hugh has that as a human being too. He lives in the present and is right there with what is happening around him, whereas, sadly, many other actors always seem to have one foot out the door toward the next job when they are rehearsing or even performing. I think audiences feel that."
~ Susan Stroman, choreographer of *Oklahoma!* in London

"It's ridiculous how wonderful this man is. I mean, the intimidation was only there before I met him. I thought, 'Oh my gosh, I'm gonna be working with a superstar.' And then you start working with him and you go, 'He's talented and good looking and charming and has integrity and work ethic.' He really is this amazing man, who has found a complete balance between personal life, professional life, stardom. I really cannot say enough good things about him. It's been an absolute pleasure and dream to work with him."
~ Stephanie Block, co-star in *The Boy from Oz*

"He is genuinely the most generous, happy, uplifting person to be around."
~ David Wenham, *Van Helsing* co-star

"You always connect immediately with whoever's talking to you, whatever moment you're going through. It's such a beautiful quality."
~ Rachel Weisz, co-star in *The Fountain*

"His positive energy really is above and beyond what I could have expected. He really taught me that it's important to be good to people. That that is the number one priority no matter what work we do is to be good to each other, to be kind to each other."
~Lynn Collins, co-star in *X-Men Origins: Wolverine*

"There's something about Hugh that is so disarming and open and charming. In his great Australian way he's not better than anybody; he's not cooler than anybody."
~ Bill Condon, producer of the Academy Awards

"I mean he's such ... you can't really say enough great things about Hugh. Everybody's just, 'Oh I heard he's the nicest guy, is it true?' And it's just like, it's beyond true. The guy is just, sets the bar. He's so well aligned in his integrity and his purpose just to ... He's such a giver, you know. It's so amazing, he's so selfless and he's so full of heart, that it's just, it kinda makes you not wanna work with anybody else."
~ Eddie Davenport, Hugh's stunt double in *Real Steel* and *Logan*

"His spirit is so special, that you understand the spirituality of Jean Valjean in a way I don't think, if you didn't have it inside you, could ever be convincingly acted."
~ Cameron Mackintosh, producer of *Les Miserables*

"Hugh makes goodness vividly interesting."
~ Tom Hooper, director of *Les Miserables*

"You are the most phenomenally talented performer, but there's not an ounce of ego inside of you. How do you do that?"
~ Anne Hathaway, co-star in *Les Miserables*

"Watching you live your life the way you do makes me want to live mine on a higher vibration."
~ Oprah Winfrey

"We just had loads of fun, and Hugh's someone I really, really, really enjoy spending time with."
~ Taron Egerton, co-star in *Eddie the Eagle*

"There's a joy to being with him. With many actors of his magnitude of stardom, there can be an aspect of their existence that's royal and apart. But that's not the way with Hugh. He's got an exuberance and unguardedness, and he talks to everybody on set. He loves life and is really grateful for the one that's been granted to him."
~ James Mangold, director of *Kate & Leopold, The Wolverine* and *Logan*

"He loves seeing the best in people and making people happy."
~ Zac Efron, *The Greatest Showman* co-star

191

"I'm so inspired by the heart of this man and his genuine generosity and grace to ALL people, as he continues to follow his dream."
~ Jeremy Hudson, dancer in *The Greatest Showman*

"Everyone knows that Hugh is a brilliant actor, and I think viewers will be impressed by his performance, which is so multi-faceted, authentic and fun. But I do not know if everyone can really appreciate how good and clever Hugh is, just by watching him in the movies. He is truly one of the most dignified, generous and fun colleagues with whom I have worked. I think everyone who works with him says the same thing."
~ Matt Bai, writer of *The Front Runner*

"I almost feel corny saying this because I'm in my twenties, but he's a role model. He's exactly how you would want somebody to behave who's leading a set. He's so full of energy, always gregarious, and one of the most committed actors I've ever worked with. And he's amazing, so great at his job."
~ Mamoudou Ali, actor in *The Front Runner*

"It's not hard to play his staffer and have this kind of hero worship and want to put everything in your heart and soul behind this guy, because that's just the sort of person that he is. The entire campaign staff on day one was like, 'I would take a bullet for that man.'"
~ Molly Ephraim, actor in *The Front Runner*

"Some people, if you can believe it, are even better in real life. This guy is one of those rare unicorns."
~ Pink

It's not just Hugh, he and Deb both have their share of raving fans.

"There are no airs and graces; they're a breath of fresh air. There's no doubt that no matter where you come from, once you're a celebrity, people start to act and behave like celebrities. They have stayed who they are."
~ Rev. Tim Costello, CEO of World Vision Australia

"Deb, you are a person with a big, big heart. When you adopt a cause you don't just skim the surface, you embrace it wholeheartedly, like you have

with the welfare of orphans around the world. You are a great friend and one of a kind."
~ Queen Rania of Jordan

"Deb is the type of person that is not overwhelmed or thrown for a loop by anything, that's what makes her so wonderful to be around. You just feel like you're with someone that can deal with anything, and I think that's a very rare quality."
~ Jerry Seinfeld

"To have Deborra-lee Furness back on the screen is just amazing, and to work with her was just such a privilege. She's incredible to work with and such an incredible woman. She's so warm and generous and supportive of everyone."
~ Zoe Ventoura, co-star in *Hyde and Seek*

"There's something about Deb's energy which just puts the biggest smile on everybody's face. If someone is a candle, I think, Deb, you're a power station! And there's something about your generosity of spirit, I think that's what sets you apart. People connected under Deb's roof – actors, musicians, artists, writers, directors, you name it."
~ Sigrid Thornton, Australian actress

"Whenever you saw Deborra-lee's name on a call sheet or on a schedule, you'd know that this day's going to be good. There's no one that I know who doesn't want to be with Deborra-lee."
~ Peter Phelps, Australian actor

You see why they are the poster kids for the Joy Revolution?
As their stature in the world has grown, they've been able to grow the scope of uplifting others as well. They're deeply involved with organizations like World Vision and Global Citizen, not to mention the groups they've started themselves: Adopt Change, Hopeland, and the Laughing Man Foundation. As Deb says, "Money is energy. It can be used for good or evil. When we start to make money, it is an opportunity to have grace, and how to know how to handle that energy." I sure like how Hugh and Deb handle what they've been given.
Hugh may credit his upbringing for his "nicest guy" persona, but I have another hypothesis. When we as humans are mean to each other, it

usually comes from a place of feeling inadequate within ourselves. Conversely, a person who is comfortable in his own skin and confident in himself finds it easy and natural to see the best in others. Hugh's secret weapon truly is Deb's unconditional love. Knowing that she accepts and adores him no matter what, has opened him up to see himself that way, too, and that is reflected in how he treats others. Deb was the recipient of that unconditional adoration from Fay, and she is passing it along to Hugh and their kids. When you give the gift of unconditional love, first to yourself, then to those closest to you, that love gets paid forward in a massive way.

When you continue to follow what lights you up, you become a power station!

CHAPTER 17

YOUNGER AND WISER

Look forward. Keep learning.

This whole book is filled with wisdom from Hugh and Deb, but I want to close by highlighting a few things I find especially impactful.

1. Don't look back, look **forward**. You can't change the past, but by looking forward and dreaming, how you feel about the past will change. You'll realize you have power to create the life you want. Enjoy where you are today, and be curious about the possibilities.
2. Be **authentic**. Be *you*. That will give you the confidence to become *more* you, to expand your comfort zone, to try new things when you want to.
3. Right *now*, be fully alive and aware. Be **connected** with those you love.
4. Articulate your dreams, then let your emotions tell you when you're **aligned** with the highest version of yourself. Joy is the real fountain of youth!

Look Forward

When Hugh turned 50, he got a lot of "When you look back..." questions—does he have any regrets, that type of thing. I LOVE his answer.

I'm someone who tries really hard to look forward—never back. I prefer to be curious about what it is you're creating rather than looking back. I know it sounds like a bumper sticker, but that's genuinely how I feel – I'm yet to hit the good or bad versions of a mid-life crisis so the number for me doesn't make me at all reflective. In fact, the people I admire the most are older, as they seem to get more curious. That's the secret to feeling young.

While traveling, he's less interested in museums and historical sites than in seeing what's NEW in each city. What's currently being created? He was philosophical about age while filming *Pan* as well. "Age is more about how you feel about life than the chronological age." He recommends reading J.M. Barrie's original *Peter Pan* book as a reminder to always keep looking at the world with a "childlike sense of wonder and magic."

Be authentically You

In reflecting on the end of *The Wolverine,* Hugh said, "He's at a point where he's relatively comfortable with who he is, and he's like 'Bring it on. Let's see what happens,' which I think is a good place for everybody to be."

There is such freedom in getting really familiar with your own inner voice and letting it be louder than the crowd around you. Hugh felt he learned a lot of that in acting school. "I think I started acting to kind of work myself out. Everyone should do this – the breathing, the learning to let go of yourself and have fun, learning to trust your instincts, not be afraid of what other people think about you, this is like a good self-help class!" If acting school isn't in your plan (like most of us), learning to be really aware of your emotions will lead you in the same direction. That's how your inner voice speaks.

The character of Wolverine has helped Hugh move in that direction. As he described it, Wolverine is "authentic—he is who he is and he doesn't pretend to be anything else, and I think I've become more like that." Hugh characterized his own journey as going from an early career theme of "I'm just a boy who can't say no," to "I don't care what you think, this is what I believe in," inspired by Wolverine.

It feels as if this gets easier as I get older. I'm writing this chapter the morning of my 47th birthday, and it's true that in each decade I've become more confident in who I am and less concerned about what other people think. Hugh was asked in 2011, when he was 43, if he still cared what people think of him. "Yes. Less than I used to. But yeah, it's there. It would be nice to be completely free of that but I'm not." Judging by his interviews as he turned 50, I would say it lessens for him as the years go by also. We're still social creatures so it probably doesn't ever go away completely. I wonder sometimes if that's what kids with autism are here to teach us. One of their gifts is giving very little attention to what other people think and expect.

When you temper yourself to try to please others, you deprive the world of your unique gifts. Something Hugh said recently about preparing for his world tour, struck me on a very profound level. He said, "The more personal and real you are, the more universal it feels to everybody." People can *feel* authenticity, and it gives them permission to relax and be authentic as well.

Deb's authenticity has continued through fame and fortune. Asked what her life is like, she replied, "It's the same as everyone's experience. It's not a Disney movie. But do I love my life? Yes." Asked if she ever has moments of self-doubt, Deb's answer is, "Daily!" But she doesn't let that slow her down. She says fame or money "is just energy." You choose how you use it.

When Deb was asked about how she's been able to create organizations that affect children on multiple continents, her answer was immediate. "I think that being true to yourself, being authentic, and doing what you want to do, has a ripple effect not only on your family and your friends, but the world at large. I think there's a lot to be said about joy and happiness and peace and creating that energy."

I couldn't have said it better myself.

Be connected

Part of the power of not looking back is that when you're alive and aware in the present moment, you're more connected with those around you. Hugh's words:

> I am a believer myself that there is a connection between every person—that's my own spiritual belief. I feel that theater, beyond the immediate form of entertainment and education, is a reminder to everyone of connection. What ironically is required is not a lot of doing but a lot of letting

go because I think a lot of it is natural. What I found when I started learning acting is I was trying so hard. [The key is] having enough confidence in yourself to be able to just let go and let the music or the story or the dialogue [happen]. Or just being with people—eye contact—and letting that establish a connection. Take away any barriers that you can.

That's one of the next areas of focus in my journey. My autopilot brain has built up momentum around me being a natural introvert and being uncomfortable in social situations. I'm not changing who I am; I still get recharged by alone time. But I'm shifting toward relaxing enough in a group of people to watch for others who have a desire to connect but might also be quieter about it. I can relate to Hugh's thought about trying too hard. So I love what he said about filming *Prisoners,* that "The more relaxed you are, the easier it is to drop into intensity of emotion."

Hugh is a deep thinker. In a January 2018 interview he was asked what book was on his bedside table. He said there were "stacks" of books there, including many about spirituality. One reason he did the *The Fountain* was because the message spoke strongly to him. The tree of the knowledge of good and evil speaks of duality and separation. And the tree of life represents oneness and our eternal nature. "Until you can accept dying, then you can't fully live," Hugh said. Deep. And true.

My own changing perception of death has made a big difference in living with more Joy. As author Charles Franklin said, "No one gets out of this life alive." When an endpoint is inevitable, it makes sense to enjoy your time to the fullest, doesn't it?

Set goals if they bring you joy, not because you have anything to prove to anyone. What if you change the definition of *success* to be experiencing more and more joyful moments? Deb is on board: "Now I'm doing things that make me happy, and being in the moment, and when you are fully present in the moment that is true happiness to me. Happiness is success."

Would you want to live forever? Of course Hugh has been asked if he'd like a taste of Wolverine's immortality. In an interview at the Chinese premiere of *The Wolverine* a few days after his 45th birthday, he had this to say:

It's not necessarily the length of your life that matters, but the quality of your life, and having a purpose, having love, people around you that you care for, that care for you. These are the things that life should be measured by, not necessarily just length. If you are offering me immortality right here, right now, I would certainly want 24 hours to think about it. (laughs) But ultimately what's more important is contentment, what you're offering the world, what the quality of your life is day by day.

Articulate your dreams

Have you sat down and thought about what your ideal day would look like? That's a powerful exercise for your journal. Katie Couric asked Hugh about his idea of a perfect day.

Waking up, massive breakfast. Actually, before breakfast going to the beach with my kids, swimming as the sun comes up. Great food, hanging out with my kids. I'm pretty boring. I love roller coasters, too, so probably like an hour of the scariest roller coasters imaginable. Did I mention sex in there somewhere? We're only up to 10 a.m....

Clearly articulating what you want is the beginning of your Joy Revolution. When you untangle the knot of *shoulds* in your head, you allow your uniqueness to shine! The things you love to do are how you make your mark. So be aware of what your emotions are telling you about your autopilot brain, reprogram it if you need to, then follow what sparks joy! When you are lit up, you can't help but light up those around you.

In summary:

"You can't get it wrong and you'll never get it done."
~Abraham Hicks

"Life is about balance. You gotta be naughty AND nice."
~Hugh Jackman

"The best is yet to come."
~Kirk Douglas, age 102

WHAT'S NEXT?

Want support as you move into your own Joy Revolution?

Connect with me on social media:

Facebook.com/LouisaforJoy
Instagram.com/LouisaforJoy

Continue the adventure:

www.JoinTheJoyRevolution.com

Join our community:

www.MyJoyRevolution.com

45211657R00116

Made in the USA
Lexington, KY
14 July 2019